PENGUIN CLASSICS

THE NARROW ROAD TO THE DEEP NORTH

ADVISORY EDITOR: BETTY RADICE

BASHŌ, the Japanese poet and diarist, was born in Iga-ueno near Kyoto in 1644. He spent his youth as companion to the son of the local lord, and with him he studied the writing of seventeen-syllable verse. In 1667 he moved to Edo (now Tokyo) where he continued to write verse. He eventually became a recluse, living on the outskirts of Edo in a hut. When he travelled he relied entirely on the hospitality of temples and fellow-poets. In his writings he was strongly influenced by the Zen sect of Buddhism.

NOBUYUKI YUASA was born in Hiroshima Prefecture in Japan in 1932. He graduated from Hiroshima University in 1954 with an English degree. He received his Master of Arts from the University of California in 1956, and continued his graduate studies at Hiroshima University. He has been teaching English at the University since 1961. He has published a number of papers in literary journals and has written a translation of Issa's *Oraga Haru*, published in 1960. .

BASHŌ

THE NARROW ROAD TO
THE DEEP NORTH

AND OTHER TRAVEL
SKETCHES

*Translated from the Japanese
with an introduction by*
NOBUYUKI YUASA

PENGUIN BOOKS

Penguin Books Ltd, 27 Wrights Lane, London w8 5tz (Publishing and Editorial)
and Harmondsworth, Middlesex, England (Distribution and Warehouse)
Viking Penguin Inc., 40 West 23rd Street, New York, New York 10010, USA
Penguin Books Australia Ltd, Ringwood, Victoria, Australia
Penguin Books Canada Ltd, 2801 John Street, Markham, Ontario, Canada l3r 1b4
Penguin Books (NZ) Ltd, 182–190 Wairau Road, Auckland 10, New Zealand

These translations first published 1966
Reprinted 1968, 1970, 1972, 1974, 1975, 1977, 1979, 1981, 1983, 1986, 1987

Made and printed in Great Britain by
Richard Clay Ltd, Bungay, Suffolk
Set in Monotype Bembo

CONTENTS

ACKNOWLEDGEMENTS

To translate from one language into another is a fearsome task. It is a fitting punishment for that human pride which led to the great confusion of languages. When the present work was but begun some three years ago, a friend of mine who happened to see me labouring over it, remarked in an innocent manner that I was attempting an impossibility. When the work was a little more advanced, a more sympathetic friend questioned whether I had the same command of English as Bashō did of the language in which he wrote. It is, therefore, with a great deal of humility and self-reproach that I am now sending the work to the press.

Through the years of assiduous work, however, I have been aided by a number of people. My deepest gratitude goes to Mr George James Moor who kindly took the trouble of reading my manuscript at different stages of its growth, always providing me with valuable suggestions not only on grammar but also on delicate points of style and composition. Without his help, it is most certain that the present work would never have gained its form. I am also indebted to Professor Kinjirō Kaneko, Professor Tadashi Iwasa, Professor Takeshi Morita and Assistant Professor Keiji Inaga for giving a greater degree of accuracy to my work by checking the names and dates with their experienced eyes. I am also grateful to Mr Rihei Okada, director of the Itsuō Museum, Ikeda City, Ōsaka, for kindly permitting me to use the portrait of Bashō and the illustrations in the text. Finally I must thank Mrs Betty Radice of Penguin Books Ltd and Mrs Nina Froud of Harvey Unna Ltd for their kind co-operation.

Hiroshima 1965   NOBUYUKI YUASA

INTRODUCTION

HAIKU, or *hokku* as it was called during the lifetime of Bashō, is the shortest among the traditionally accepted forms of Japanese poetry. It consists of seventeen syllables,[1] divided into three sections of five–seven–five. For example,

Furuike ya, kawazu tobikomu, mizu no oto.

> Breaking the silence
> Of an ancient pond,
> A frog jumped into water –
> A deep resonance.[2]

It is obvious, however, that it is not sufficient to define *haiku* purely from the standpoint of syllabic structure, for *haiku*, like any other form in literature, has grown out of a long process, and it is subject to a number of restrictions historically imposed upon it. Let me, therefore, attempt by way of introduction a short history of *haiku* so that the reader may get acquainted with the essential traits of this most fascinating literary form.

Long before *haiku*, or even its distant prototype, came into existence, there was already an established form of poetry in Japanese literature, and this form, *waka*, consisted of thirty-one syllables, divided into five sections of five–seven–five–seven–seven. For example,

Haru no no ni, sumire tsumi ni to, ko shi ware zo,
no o natsukashimi, hitoyo ne ni keru.

> Coming with a light heart
> To pick some violets,

9

I found it difficult to leave
And slept overnight
Here in this spring field.[3]

Or again,

*Hisakata no, hikari nodokeki, haru no hi ni,
shizugokoro naku, hana no chiru ramu.*

On a long spring day,
When all is happily bathed
In the peaceful sun,
Cherry blossoms alone fall –
Unwilling to stay?[4]

As these examples indicate, this older and longer form of
Japanese poetry was particularly suited for emotive ex-
pression and refined description of nature. Hence it became
extremely popular among aristocratic courtiers. Courtiers,
however, employed this form sometimes in their playful
mood as a medium of witty conversation, breaking it into
two separate halves of five–seven–five and seven–seven.
For example,

Okuyama ni, fune kogu oto no, kikoyuru wa.

Nareru konomi ya, umi wataru ramu.

How is it that I hear
The noise of creaking oars
In the deepest mountains?

Because of the ripening fruits
That rub against wood as oars do.[5]

Or again,

> *Hitogokoro, ushimitsu ima wa, tanoma ji yo.*
> *Yume ni miyu ya to, ne zo sugi ni keru.*
>
>> It has passed midnight,
>> I no longer wait for you,
>> Pining for sorrow.
>>
>> Oh, dear, I overslept,
>> Wanting to see you in the dream.[6]

Sometimes the order of the two halves was reversed to give more independence to each counterpart and greater freedom to the exercise of wit. For example,

> *Ta ni hamu koma wa, kuro ni zo ari keru.*
> *Nawashiro no, mizu ni wa kage to, mie tsure do.*
>
>> The horse grazing on the bank
>> Seems to me black in colour.
>>
>> I think it otherwise,
>> For its reflection in the paddy
>> Says chestnut-brown.[7]

This kind of witty verse, which continued to be written under the name of linked verse (*renga*) throughout the Heian period (794–1191), seems to me to be the earliest germ of *haiku* poetry, for it is here that for the first time the five–seven–five syllabic structure came to be recognized as a poetic unit, though not completely independent, and furthermore, the witty and playful tone of the linked verse is a heritage which passes into the marrow of later *haiku*, though somewhat modified by subsequent developments.

Towards the end of the Heian period, and more

universally in the Kamakura period (1192–1392), arose the fashion of writing a long chain of linked verse by multiplying the number of links. For example,

> *Nara no miyako o, omoi koso yare.*
>
> *Yaezakura, aki no momiji ya, ika nara mu.*
>
> *Shigururu tabi ni, iro ya kasanaru.*

> I wonder how it is now
> In the ancient capital of Nara.

> Those time-honoured cherries
> That bloom in double flowers
> Must be in their autumnal tints.

> Each rain of fall brings forth
> Ever-deepening colours in the leaves.[8]

In the beginning, the number of poems thus linked together was relatively small, but before long as many as thirty-six, forty-four, fifty, or even one hundred poems began to be included in a series. What must be borne in mind in reading these long sequences of linked verse is that they were written by a number of poets sitting together and writing alternately, and that each poem in a series was linked to the immediately preceding one either by witty association or verbal play. The result was often a kind of kaleidoscopic beauty with infinite variety revealed to the reader in a slowly evolving movement.

Inherent in these long sequences of linked verse, however, was a danger that they might degenerate into chaotic confusion or tedious monotony. To prevent this, therefore, various attempts were made to establish certain rules of composition, and various schools of poets began to be formed. During the Kamakura period, these schools were classified roughly into two groups, serious (*ushin*) and non-serious (*mushin*), the former trying to emulate the elegant style of *waka* and the latter persisting in witty composition of a lower order. Towards the end of the Kamakura period and during the Muromachi period (1393–1602), however, the poets of the serious group won gradual ascendancy, and with the coming of Sōgi (1421–1502) the art of linked verse reached its perfection. Let me quote here the first eight poems of his masterpiece called *Minase Sangin* as an example of his superb art.

> Snow-capped as they are,
> The gentle slopes of the mountains
> Fade into the hazy mist
> At twilight on a spring day.

> The river descends far and distant,
> Plum-fragrance filling the village.

> In a soft river breeze
> Stands a single willow tree
> Fresh in spring colour.

> At early dawn every push of the oar
> Is audible from a passing boat.

> There must be a moon
> Dying in the morning sky
> Wrapped in a heavy fog.

> The ground is covered with frost,
> The autumn is drawing to its close.

In a sorrowful voice
A cricket is heard singing
Beneath the withering grass.

I paid a call to a friend of mine,
Taking a desolate lane by the hedge.[9]

Note in the above how each poem takes up the suggestion of the preceding poem and yet opens a new world of its own, so that the reader is carried through the whole series as through the exquisitely arranged rooms of a building, always entertained by delightful changes but never arrested by sudden contradictions. It is no longer witty association or verbal play but something in the depths of the human heart that combines these poems. I think it is particularly significant from our point of view that already in the times of Sōgi, the starting piece (*hokku*) of a series, which was always written in the five–seven–five syllable form, was given a special place and composed only by the most experienced of the poets. At least two things were considered essential to the starting piece. First, a reference to the season in which it is written, and second, the existence of the so-called breaking word (*kireji*), a short emotionally charged word which, by arresting the flow of poetic statement for a moment, gives extra strength and dignity. These are restrictions that bind later *haiku* as well.

Towards the end of the Muromachi period and in the early part of the Edo period (1603–1866), linked verse of a lower order (*haikai no renga*), which continued to be written in the preceding age merely as a kind of recreative pastime, gained enormous popularity. This is, of course, partly due to the over-refinement and elaboration of serious poetry, but mainly because freedom and open laughter, which characterized linked verse of a lower order, suited the taste of the merchant class which was then rising throughout the country. The earliest innovators are Sōkan (dates unknown) and Moritake (1473–1549). Let me quote here some of their poems (*hokku*) to give a glimpse of their poetic world.

> In a perfect circle
> Rises the spring day,
> But it gains an enormous length
> By the time it sinks.

> To the moon in the sky
> If you put a handle,
> It will certainly be
> An excellent fan.

> A hanging willow
> In beautiful green
> Paints eyebrows
> On the brow of a cliff.

> Not in the flower
> But rather in the nose
> The smell resides –
> So it seems to me.

Even in the technique of linking, they seem to have almost gone back to the playful mood of the poets of the Heian period. For example,

> I wanted, yet not quite wanted,
> To use my sword to kill a man.

> Capturing a thief,
> I was surprised to find him
> None but my own son.[10]

Or again,

> Lighter than paper,
> Plum blossoms are sent flying
> In the holy compound
> On a spring day.
>
> Unwilling it seems, to fall behind,
> Crows and bush warblers fly about.[11]

The witticism of Sōkan and Moritake was carried a step further to a bold and conscious acceptance of colloquialism by Teitoku (1571–1653). He it was who first stated explicitly that linked verse of a lower order had an artistic merit peculiar to itself, and that it, being 'the voice of the happy people', should not hesitate to use any popular terminology (*haigon*) available to provoke healthy laughter. What actually happened in his poetry, however, was somewhat different from what he proposed to do in his theoretical statements, for he did everything so consciously, so calculatingly: almost by rule and measure. For example,

> Wonderful coolness
> Is packed intact
> In the lumpish moon
> Of a summer evening.
>
> No bigger than a fist, it seems,
> The clouds that brought the shower.[12]

This linked verse happens to be fairly good poetry, but if one looks at it closely, one realizes that the link is provided by an elaborate net of verbal association ('lump' and 'fist,' and 'evening' and 'shower'). Bashō criticized this kind of linking technique as being mechanical (*mono-zuke*), for, carried to an extreme, it often leads to the impoverishment of poetry. The same tendency can be detected in Teitoku's *hokku*.

> Dumplings rather than flowers
> They seem to choose –
> Those wild geese
> Flying home to the north.

> The year of the tiger
> Has come –
> Even the spring mist rises
> In spots and stripes.

What Teitoku intended but did not quite succeeed in doing, was achieved by Sōin (1605–82) and his disciples, particularly Saikaku (1642–93) among them. I think it is significant that both Sōin and Saikaku chose as the centre of their activity Ōsaka, the city where the power of the merchant class was strongest. In the poems of Teitoku, as we have seen, the language was often colloquial enough, but the depicted scenes themselves were not greatly different from the elegant scenes of serious poetry. In the poems of Sōin and Saikaku, however, all the events of this 'floating world' are reported with absolute freedom – in cheerful rhythm and truly popular idiom. To quote some of their *hokku*:

> Long rain of May,
> The whole world is
> A single sheet of paper
> Under the clouds.

Exactly in the shape of
A letter in the Dutch alphabet
Lies in the sky
A band of wild geese.

Saying, 'Shishi, shishi,'
My wife encourages the baby
To pass water, and I hear
The noise of a morning shower.

Walking in a desolate field,
I picked up a woman's comb;
She must have come here
To pluck flowers in spring.

Sōin and his disciples insisted that the real merit of their poetry was in metaphor (*gūgen*), that is, saying one thing and meaning another. This is an idea that was later developed by Bashō into the more significant theory of substance (*jitsu*) and essence (*kyo*) in poetry. As interpreted by Sōin and his disciples, however, metaphor meant simply bringing together two things of different categories by ingenuity. For example, a morning shower and urination in the third poem quoted above. The same kind of ingenious flight can be detected in the linking technique.

Thus gathered in a company,
We have in the midst of us
A tree of laughter and talk,
A fragrant plum tree.

The piercing voice of a bush warbler
Is an alarm for the slumbering world.

> On a misty morning,
> A line of smoke from my pipe
> Is broken sideways.
>
> Palanquin-bearers having passed,
> There arose a blast of mountain wind.[13]

Here the links are provided by clever interpretation and ingenious transfer (what Bashō called *kokoro-zuke*). It was certainly an improvement over the mechanical linking technique of Teitoku, because it opened a new world of poetry by giving a freer play to the human mind. There was, however, something vitally important lacking in the poetry of Sōin and his disciples, as is amply testified by their inferior works which almost degenerated into nonsense verse. Just when people became aware of this – when poets like Gonsui (1650–1722) and Onitsura (1661–1738) were making their efforts to save poetry from vulgarity – our master, Matsuo Bashō (1644–94) employed his great genius to lift *haiku* once and for all into the realm of perfect poetry: poetry that embodied in itself at once the seriousness and elegance of Sōgi and the freedom and energy of Sōin, indeed, poetry that is worth reading hundreds of years after his death, or for that matter, at any time in human history.

Bashō was born in the city of Ueno in the province of Iga (now a part of Mie Prefecture) in 1644. His father, Yozaemon, was a minor *samurai* in the service of the Tōdō family that had ruled the city for a number of generations. Bashō had two elder brothers, and one elder and three younger sisters. Financially, his family was not particularly favoured, and his father is said to have supported the family by teaching writing to the children of the vicinity. Bashō was called Kinsaku in childhood, and Tōshichirō, or sometimes Chūemon, after his coming of age. In 1653, when Bashō was only nine years old, he entered the service of the Tōdō family, officially as a page, but in reality more as a study-mate of the young heir, Yoshitada, who was older than Bashō by only two years. Thus began their relatively short but extremely warm friendship. In 1655 Bashō's father died.

Born with a delicate constitution, Yoshitada took more to the acquisition of literary accomplishments than to the practice of military arts. He and Bashō studied the art of linked verse under the guidance of Kigin (1624–1705), one of the ablest disciples of Teitoku. Yoshitada must have been a fairly good poet himself, for he was given the pen name of Sengin, which had one character in common with his teacher's pen name. Bashō's pen name in those days was Sōbō. The following two poems (*hokku*) of his, published in 1664 in the anthology named *Sayono-nakayama Shū*, are the earliest recorded.

> The moon is the guide,
> Come this way to my house,
> So saying, invites
> The host of a wayside inn.

> The leafless cherry,
> Old as a toothless woman,
> Blooms in flowers,
> Mindful of its youth.

Needless to say, one can detect a heavy influence of the deliberate style of Teitoku in these poems. In 1665 Sengin, together with his fellow poets, composed a chain of linked verse consisting of one hundred pieces to commemorate the thirteenth anniversary of Teitoku's death. Bashō contributed seventeen poems, but they were written in a style quite similar to that of the poems quoted above.

In 1666 Sengin died at the age of twenty-five. His early and sudden death must have given Bashō a tremendous shock, for upon returning from Kōyasan, where he enshrined the mortuary tablet of Sengin by the order of the bereaved father, Bashō asked for permission to resign from his service. The permission denied, he ran away to Kyōto.

The exact manner in which Bashō spent the next five years in Kyōto is unknown. It is generally believed, however, that, making his abode at the Kinpukuji Temple, he studied Japanese classics under Kigin, Chinese classics under Itō Tanan, and calligraphy under Kitamuki Unchiku. One can detect an air of greater freedom in the poems Bashō wrote during his stay in Kyōto. For example,

> Unable to meet
> At their annual rendezvous,
> The two stars fret
> In the fretful sky of July.

> Coquettish bush-clovers
> Stretched out on the ground,
> Ill-mannered just as much
> As they are beautiful.

> The sharp-crying cuckoo
> Seems to have dyed
> With the blood of his mouth
> These azaleas on the rocks.

The episode with Juteini is also believed to be an event of those years. Historically, however, there is nothing known about this woman except that she was the mistress of Bashō in his youthful days. In any case, the five years in Kyōto must have been very fruitful and yet in many ways stormy ones for Bashō.

In 1671 Bashō returned to his native place, and in the spring of the following year, he presented to the Tenman Shrine of Ueno City the first anthology of his own editing, named *Kai Ōi*. It was a collection of *hokku* coupled in pairs, each pair compared, judged and criticized by Bashō. For example,

> Time and time again,
> Nipped by a sickle
> With a click –
> Beautiful, beautiful cherry.

> Come and take a look
> At this tapestry of cherry,
> Tapestry-coated old man,
> My friend, Jinbe.

The first poem, by Rosetu,[14] is excellent in that it praises the cherry tree by saying, 'Time and time again'. Wit of this kind is certainly a model for all composition. The second poem by myself, tries to communicate the idea that Jinbe's rich coat will lose its colour, if he comes to see the cherry. It must be admitted, however, that this poem is weak not only in structure but also in diction that gives real beauty to the poem. Let me condemn my poem therefore, by saying that Jinbe's soft head is no match for the sharp blade of the sickle.

It is possible, of course, to suspect that this judgement was

formed by Bashō out of the modesty which was so charac-
teristic of him, but at the same time, no one will fail to
observe that this anthology was the work of a very ambi-
tious man. So in 1672, after a short stay of several months
in his native place, Bashō left for Edo (Tōkyō), the city
which was thriving as the seat of the Tokugawa govern-
ment. His firm determination at the time of departure is
expressed by the poem he left behind.

> Separated we shall be
> For ever, my friends,
> Like the wild geese
> Lost in the clouds.

Now, unlike Kyōto, Edo was a relatively young and
growing city, and there was a great deal of activity and
freedom in the air. For the first few years at least, Bashō
seems to have found it difficult to decide what he really
wanted to do. He stayed with his friends and admirers, and
engaged in work of a miscellaneous character. Even
through those years of groping, however, Bashō seems to
have gained an increasingly firm footing in the poetic
circles of Edo, for in 1675 when Sōin came from Ōsaka,
Bashō was among the poets who were invited to compose
linked verse with him.

The encounter with Sōin must have been an epoch-
making event for Bashō, for upon this occasion he changed
his pen name from Sōbō to Tōsei. Deep respect for Sōin,
as well as his marked influence, can be felt in the linked
verse he composed in the year after.

> Under this plum tree,
> Even a black bull will learn

To sing a song of spring
Filled with cheerful joy.

Coming, as it is, from a human throat,
The song is better than the frog's chorus.

Lightly, fancifully,
Sprinkled upon this world –
Tiny rains of spring.

In the field, young shoots float in pools
Muddy as bean-paste mixed with vinegar.[15]

Note in the above the absolute freedom of movement which was typical of Sōin and his school. In the first poem, Bashō identifies himself with a black bull and admires the plum tree which is the source of his poetic inspiration, namely Sōin. In the second poem, one of the Bashō's disciples praises him for writing a beautiful song. What Bashō learned from Sōin is the special value in poetry of the humble and unpretentious imagery of everyday life, as he himself testifies by saying,

If you describe a green willow in the spring rain it will be excellent as linked verse of a higher order. Linked verse of a lower order, however, must use more homely images, such as a crow picking mud-snails in a rice paddy.

Bashō is reported to have said, 'But for Sōin, we would be still licking the slaver of aged Teitoku.'

In the summer of 1676, Bashō returned to his native place for a short visit – with the following poem.

My souvenir from Edo
Is the refreshingly cold wind
Of Mount Fuji
I brought home on my fan.

Returning to Edo almost immediately, he actively engaged in writing poetry. During the following four years, his poems were published in different anthologies in large numbers, and also anthologies consisting mainly of his and his disciples' poems began to be published, among which *Edo Sangin*, *Tōsei Montei Dokugin Nijū Kasen*, *Inaka no Kuawase*, and *Tokiwaya no Kuawase* may be mentioned. On the whole, however, Bashō's poems of this period reflect the playful tone and ingenious style of Sōin. To quote some of them:

> A male cat
> Passed through the hole
> In the broken hearth
> To meet his mistress.

> So it was all right,
> Yesterday has passed safely,
> Though I ate and drank
> Quantities of globefish soup.

> Ah, it is spring,
> Great spring it is now,
> Great, great spring –
> Ah, great –

Bashō, however, was not satisfied to remain in this kind of low-toned atmosphere of the 'floating world' for long. There was something in him which gradually rebelled against it. In 1680, Sampū,[16] one of the admirers of Bashō, built for him a small house in Fukagawa, not far from the River Sumida, in a relatively isolated spot. In the winter of the same year, a stock of Bashō tree (a certain species of banana tree) was presented to him by one of his disciples.

Bashō seems to have felt a special attachment to this tree from the very beginning, for he says:

> I planted in my garden
> A stock of Bashō tree,
> And hated at once
> The shooting bush-clovers.

Or again about the same tree, he wrote in later years:

The leaves of the Bashō tree are large enough to cover a harp. When they are wind-broken, they remind me of the injured tail of a phoenix, and when they are torn, they remind me of a green fan ripped by the wind. The tree does bear flowers, but unlike other flowers, there is nothing gay about them. The big trunk of the tree is untouched by the axe, for it is utterly useless as building wood. I love the tree, however, for its very uselessness . . . I sit underneath it, and enjoy the wind and rain that blow against it.

This must have been another epoch-making event for Bashō, for it is from this tree that he took a name for his house, and eventually a new pen name for himself.

Bashō's life at his riverside house must have been an externally peaceful but internally agonizing one, for as he sat there meditating all by himself, he began to revolt more and more from the world which surrounded him. Signs of tremendous spiritual suffering are seen in the poems collected in *Azuma Nikki*, *Haikai Jiin*, and *Musashi Buri*, which were published shortly after his removal to the riverside house. To quote some of them:

> A black crow
> Has settled himself
> On a leafless tree,
> Fall of an autumn day.

At midnight
Under the bright moon,
A secret worm
Digs into a chestnut.

On a snowy morning,
I sat by myself
Chewing tough strips
Of dried salmon.

Tonight, the wind blowing
Through the Bashō tree,
I hear the leaking rain
Drop against a basin.

Oars hit waves,
And my intestines freeze,
As I sit weeping
In the dark night.

It was also during those years of suffering that Bashō came to know the Priest Bucchō[17] and practised Zen meditation under his guidance. Whether Bashō was able to attain the state of complete enlightenment is a matter open to question, for he repeatedly tells us that he has one foot in the other world and the other foot in this one. There is little doubt, however, that this opportunity gave him the power to see this world in a context in which he had never seen it before.

In 1682, when Bashō's house was only two years old, it was destroyed by a fire that swept through a large part of Edo. So Bashō sought a temporary abode in the house of Rokuso Gohei[18] at the village of Hatsukari in the province of Kai (now a part of Yamanashi Prefecture). This misfortune must have shaken him considerably, for something almost like despair is heard in the poems collected in *Minashi Guri* (*Empty Chestnut*) which was published immediately after his return to Edo in the summer of 1683. To quote from it:

> Tired of cherry,
> Tired of this whole world,
> I sit facing muddy *sake*
> And black rice.

> Who could it possibly be
> That mourns the passing autumn,
> Careless of the wind
> Rustling his beard?

> With frozen water
> That tastes painfully bitter
> A sewer rat relieves in vain
> His parched throat.

But despair is hardly the word to express the state of Bashō's mind through those years, for those were the years of the deepest meditation and severest self-scrutiny which developed his awareness of an important truth. It is best expressed by his own words.

What is important is to keep our mind high in the world of true understanding, and returning to the world of our daily experience to seek therein the truth of beauty. No matter what we may be doing at a given moment, we must not forget that it has a bearing upon our everlasting self which is poetry.

This is easy to say but difficult to practise. The poems Bashō wrote during the period 1680–83 are not entirely free

from the overtones of the ingenious style of Sōin, but they
point to the direction in which Bashō was moving – all by
himself, finding his way, step by step, through his own
suffering, with no one to guide him.

In the summer of 1683, Bashō's mother died in his native
place, and in the winter of the same year, a new house was
built for him in Fukagawa by his friends and disciples. On
this occasion Bashō wrote as follows:

> Overhearing the hail,
> My old self sits again
> In the new house,
> Like an overgrown oak.

Bashō, however, did not stay in this house for long, for
in the summer of 1684, he started on the first of his major
journeys. A vivid account of this journey is given in *The
Record of a Weather-exposed Skeleton* (*Nozarashi Kikō*), the
first of the travel sketches translated in this book, and his
route is indicated in Map 1 (p. 145).

What must be borne in mind in reading the travel
sketches by Bashō is that travels in his day had to be made
under very precarious conditions, and that few people, if
any, thought of taking to the road merely for pleasure or
pastime. Furthermore, as I have already indicated, Bashō
had been going through agonizing stages of self-scrutiny in
the years immediately preceding the travels, so that it was
quite certain that, when he left his house, he thought there
was no other alternative before him. To put it more pre-
cisely, Bashō had been casting away his earthly attachments,
one by one, in the years preceding the journey, and now he
had nothing else to cast away but his own self which was in

him as well as around him. He had to cast this self away, for otherwise he was not able to restore his true identity (what he calls the 'everlasting self which is poetry' in the passage above). He saw a tenuous chance of achieving his final goal in travelling, and he left his house 'caring naught for his provisions in the state of sheer ecstasy'.

This tragic sense is given beautiful expression in the opening passage of *The Records of a Weather-exposed Skeleton*. Viewed as a whole, however, this work is not a complete success, because there is still too much self forced upon it – because now and then crude personal emotions hinder the reader from entering into the world of its poetry. It is written in *haibun*, prose mixed with *haiku*, but the two are not perfectly amalgamated. Sometimes prose is a mere explanatory note for *haiku*, and sometimes *haiku* stands isolated from prose. Particularly towards the end of the work, prose seems to be almost forgotten. In spite of these defects, however, the work is amply rewarding to those who read it with care, because it is the work of a man who tries to cast his own self away and almost achieves it – because here and there in the work we find beautiful poems and prose passages where the author seems to have found for a brief moment his true identity. Indeed, *The Records of a Weather-exposed Skeleton* is the first work of Bashō where we find glimpses of his mature style.

Bashō returned to his home in Edo in the summer of 1685 after about nine months of wandering. In 1684, while he was still in Nagoya, however, an anthology of great importance was published. It was called *Fuyu no Hi* (*A Winter Day*), and it constitutes the first of the so-called *Seven Major Anthologies of Bashō* (*Bashō Shichibu Shū*). If one compares the linked verse of this anthology with the linked verse (quoted above) Bashō wrote back in 1676 under the influence of Sōin, one realizes the great spiritual distance he had travelled in less than a decade.

> With a bit of madness in me,
> Which is poetry,
> I plod along like Chikusai
> Among the wails of the wind.
>
> Who is it that runs with hurried steps,
> Flowers of sasanqua dancing on his hat?
>
> Under the pale sky of dawn,
> I importuned a water official
> To pose as a tavern keeper.
>
> A customer having arrived, his red horse
> Stands shaking his head moist with dew.[19]

About the special features of Bashō's linking technique I shall have more to say later. Note here, however, the sweet elegance with which the whole poem moves. The influence of Sōin is still faintly detectable, but ingenuity has given place to something at once deeper and quieter – something which is probably best described as human wisdom.

In 1686 two anthologies, *Kawazu Awase* (*Frog Contest*) and *Haru no Hi* (*A Spring Day*), were published. The former is a collection of poems on frogs by Bashō and his disciples. The latter is traditionally counted as the second of the *Major Anthologies*, though there are only three poems of Bashō in it. The importance of these anthologies rests on a single poem by Bashō included in them, which is probably the best known of all his poems. It has already been quoted at the beginning of the introduction, but let me quote it here once again with a comment by one of his disciples.[20]

> Breaking the silence
> Of an ancient pond,
> A frog jumped into water –
> A deep resonance.

This poem was written by our master on a spring day. He was sitting in his riverside house in Edo, bending his ears to the soft cooing of a pigeon in the quiet rain. There was a mild wind in the air, and one or two petals of cherry blossom were falling gently to the ground. It was the kind of day you often have in late March – so perfect that you want it to last for ever. Now and then in the garden was heard the sound of frogs jumping into the water. Our master was deeply immersed in meditation, but finally he came out with the second half of the poem,

> A frog jumped into water –
> A deep resonance.

One of the disciples[21] sitting with him immediately suggested for the first half of the poem,

> Amidst the flowers
> Of the yellow rose.

Our master thought for a while, but finally he decided on

> Breaking the silence
> Of an ancient pond.

The disciple's suggestion is admittedly picturesque and beautiful but our master's choice, being simpler, contains more truth in it. It is only he who has dug deep into the mystery of the universe that can choose a phrase like this.

So many people in the past have commented upon this poem that it seems to me that its poetic resources have been well-nigh exhausted. Still it is possible, I believe, to use this poem as an illustration of Bashō's mature style. What is remarkable in this poem is, in my opinion, the symbolism which it achieves without pretending in the least to be symbolic. On the surface the poem describes an action of the frog and its after-effects – a perfect example of objectivity. But if you meditate long enough upon the poem, you will discover that the action thus described is not merely an external one, that it also exists internally, that the pond is, indeed, a mirror held up to reflect the author's mind. Bashō explains this himself in the following way.

Go to the pine if you want to learn about the pine, or to the bamboo if you want to learn about the bamboo. And in doing so, you must leave your subjective preoccupation with yourself. Otherwise you impose yourself on the object and do not learn. Your poetry issues of its own accord when you and the object have become one – when you have plunged deep enough into the object to see something like a hidden glimmering there. However well phrased your poetry may be, if your feeling is not natural – if the object and yourself are separate – then your poetry is not true poetry but merely your subjective counterfeit.

Some people have spoken as if Bashō entered into the realization of this principle the very moment he wrote the frog poem. It is difficult to believe that it was so. On the other hand, it would hardly be an exaggeration to say that all the poems written by Bashō in his mature style are based on this principle, for it was exactly what Bashō had in mind when he said that there was a permanent, unchangeable element (*fueki*) in all poetry. In any case, crude personification

and ingenious self-dramatization have completely dis-
appeared from his poems. To quote three more:

> Under the bright moon
> I walked round and round
> The lake –
> All night long.

> Build a fire, my friend,
> So it will crackle.
> I will show you something good,
> A big ball of snow.

> All the livelong day
> A lark has sung in the air,
> Yet he seems to have had
> Not quite his fill.

In the early autumn of 1687, Bashō left on a short trip to
the Kashima Shrine. The records of this trip constitute *A
Visit to the Kashima Shrine* (*Kashima Kikō*), the second of the
travel sketches translated in this book. Although this is an
extremely short work, it is carefully organized with a
climax (rather an anti-climax, for Bashō beguiles the reader
in his own ironic way) falling just where prose ends and
poetry begins in the middle of the work. Its somewhat
religious atmosphere is due to the fact that it is a kind of
tribute to the priest Bucchō with whom Bashō studied
Zen. In its quiet beauty and also in its pseudo-archaic
flavour, this work occupies a unique position among the
travel sketches by Bashō.

Almost immediately after he returned home from his
trip to the Kashima Shrine, Bashō left on the second of his
major journeys. This time he stayed on the road for about

eleven months, following nearly the same route as he did in the first journey (for the details of his route, see Map 2, p. 146). This expedition resulted in two travel sketches, *The Records of a Travel-worn Satchel* (*Oi no Kobumi*) and *A Visit to Sarashina Village* (*Sarashina Kikō*), the third and fourth of the travel sketches translated in this book. The former covers the first half of the journey from Edo to Suma, and the latter is an account of the detour he made to the Sarashina Village (now a part of Nagano Prefecture) on his way home.

Viewed from an artistic point of view, *The Records of a Travel-worn Satchel* is a great advance over his previous travel sketches, for here for the first time an attempt was made to bring prose and *haiku* into an organic whole. When Bashō left on the journey of *The Records of the Weather-exposed Skeleton*, as I have already pointed out, he was just coming out of the agonizing years of self-scrutiny, and was busy finding his identity in nature. In *The Records of a Travel-worn Satchel*, however, he seems to have succeeded in maintaining a certain artistic distance between himself and his materials. That is why we find in it such beautiful passages as the description of the Suma Beach at the end of the book, superb indeed for its tragi-comical effect. The book is not, however, without its flaws. For one thing, Bashō writes too much *about* the travel – why he has taken to the road, how he wants to write the travel sketch, and so on. These statements, of course, have their own value, especially read as sources of critical and biographical interest. They do not necessarily, however, contribute to the total effect of the work. It seems to me that there is an air of an '*étude*' about *The Records of a Travel-worn Satchel*, and that it should be read as a kind of stepping-stone for the subsequent travel sketches.

A Visit to Sarashina Village is the shortest of all travel sketches by Bashō. It carries on, however, the wonderful tragi-comical effect of the concluding passages of *The Records of a Travel-worn Satchel*. In its fine polish, in particular, it is unrivalled and shines forth like a gem.

Bashō returned from his expedition to Suma and Sarashina in the autumn of 1688, and already in the spring of the following year he left on the third of his major journeys. Shortly before his departure, however, *Arano* (*Desolate Wilds*), the third of the *Major Anthologies*, was published. Bashō's poems included in this anthology reveal the unusual depth of mind he had achieved after a year of wandering on the road. For example,

> How amusing at first
> How melancholy it was later
> To see a cormorant show
> On the darkening river.

> Confined to my house
> By winter weather,
> I snuggled as before
> Against an old pillar.

Bashō's third major journey brought him *The Narrow Road to the Deep North* (*Oku no Hosomichi*), the last of the travel sketches translated in this book. Leaving Edo in the spring of 1689, he spent more than two and a half years on the road (see Map 3, p. 147). It is significant, I believe, that he had sold his house in Edo prior to his departure, for it means that he did not expect to return from this journey.

What is more significant, however, is that he went to the North this time, avoiding the familiar Tōkaidō route. In the imagination of the people at least, the North was largely an unexplored territory, and it represented for Bashō all the mystery there was in the universe. In other words, the Narrow Road to the Deep North was life itself for Bashō, and he travelled through it as anyone would travel through the short span of his life here – seeking a vision of eternity in the things that are, by their own very nature, destined to perish. In short, *The Narrow Road to the Deep North* is Bashō's study in eternity, and in so far as he has succeeded in this attempt, it is also a monument he has set up against the flow of time.

It seems to me that there are two things remarkable about *The Narrow Road to the Deep North*. One is variety. Each locality, including the little unknown places Bashō visited in passing, is portrayed with a distinctive character of its own, so that it is hardly an exaggeration to say that Bashō was in possession of a magical power to enter into 'the spirit of place'. Even the people he met on the road are given characters, each different from the others, so that they leave enduring impressions on the imagination of the reader. Furthermore, we often find in reading *The Narrow Road to the Deep North* themes and subjects of his previous travel sketches recurring – modified to fit a new pattern, of course, but used to create that enormous variety which alone can give the work an illusion of being as large as the universe and as infinite as time itself.

The other remarkable thing about *The Narrow Road to the Deep North* is its unity. To use Bashō's own classification, variety, being the temporary, changeable element (*ryūkō*), is in the substance (*jitsu*) of the work. Unity, on the other hand, is the permanent, unchangeable element existing in the essence (*kyo*) of the work. In other words, unity is invisible on the surface, but it is the hidden vital force that shapes the work into a meaningful whole. In *The Narrow Road to the Deep North*, we often find that even place-names are made to contribute to the total effect. Indeed the whole structure of the work is so determined as to meet the demands of unity. Take the major events of the journey, for example. They are arranged not simply linearly according to chronological sequence, but also circularly, according to time of another sort, as is demonstrated in the following table, where the events on the left half of the circle must be related to the opposing events on the right half of the circle.

This is, of course, a simplification, and the work as a whole does not present neat regularity like this. Nevertheless, anyone who reads the work with care will not fail to notice the tremendous effort Bashō makes to achieve unity through variety. Scholars have pointed out that in his attempt to achieve unity Bashō took such liberty as to change the natural course of events, or even invent fictitious events. The result is a superb work of art where unity dominates without destroying variety.

Just one more thing need be mentioned about *The*

Narrow Road to the Deep North. In his preceding travel sketches, as I have already pointed out, Bashō failed to maintain an adequate balance between prose and *haiku*, making prose subservient to *haiku*, or *haiku* isolated from prose. In the present travel sketch, however, Bashō has mastered the art of writing *haibun* so completely that prose and *haiku* illuminate each other like two mirrors held up facing each other. This is something no one before him was able to achieve, and for this reason, *The Narrow Road to the Deep North* is counted as one of the classics of Japanese literature.

Bashō travelled the great arc of the northern routes (Ōshūkaidō and Hokurikudō) in six months, arriving in Ōgaki in the autumn of 1689. This is where the record of *The Narrow Road to the Deep North* breaks off. Bashō, however, did not return to Edo till the winter of 1691. He spent this two-year period travelling a great deal in the vicinity of his native place, making short but happy sojourns at the houses of his disciples. Among such houses, Genjūan (the Vision-inhabited House) and Mumyōan (the House of Anonymity), both situated not far from Lake Biwa, and Rakushisha (the House of Fallen Persimmons) in the suburbs of Kyōto, should be mentioned. Of the last, Bashō wrote as follows:

The retreat of my disciple, Kyorai,[22] is in the suburbs of Kyōto, among the bamboo thickets of Shimo Saga – not far from either Mount Arashiyama or the Ōigawa River. It is an ideal place for meditation, for it is hushed in silence. Such is the laziness of my friend, Kyorai, that his windows are covered with tall grass growing rank in the garden, and his roofs are buried under the branches of overgrown persimmon trees. The house has developed a number of leaks, and the long rain of May has made straw mats and paper screens terribly mouldy, so that it is difficult to find a place to lie down. Ironically, the sun reaching into the house is the gift with which the master of the house welcomes his guest. I wrote:

> Long rain of May,
> I saw on the clay wall
> A square mark of writing paper
> Torn recently off.

Bashō wrote an equally beautiful *Essay on the Vision-in-habited House* (*Genjūan no Ki*), and *Saga Diary* (*Saga Nikki*) was also a product of his stay at Rakushisha.

During the two-year period we are now dealing with, two anthologies of great importance were published. They are *Hisago* (*A Gourd*) and *Saru Mino* (*A Coat for a Monkey*), the fourth and fifth of the *Major Anthologies*. The former is a slim volume consisting of five linked verses, but the latter is a large collection of some four hundred poems (*hokku*) plus four linked verses and the *Essay on the Vision-inhabited House*, and it is generally believed that those two anthologies demonstrate the mature style of Bashō (*shōfū*) at its highest pitch. To quote some poems (*hokku*) from this period:

> A man's voice piercing
> Through the air,
> The northern stars echo
> A beating fulling-block.

> In the first shower
> Of early winter,
> Even a monkey seems to crave
> For a raincoat.

Introduction

Under a cherry tree,
Soup, salad, and all else
Are brought to us,
Dressed in gay blossoms.

With a friend in Ōmi
I sat down, and bid farewell
To the departing spring,
Most reluctantly.

If nothing else,
I have this tree at least
To take shelter in –
A pasania in summer.

Hardly a hint
Of their early death,
Cicadas singing
In the trees.

Under the bright moon,
The children of the vicinity
All lined up
On the porch of a temple.

A sick stray goose
Falling into cold darkness,
I slumbered by myself –
A night on the journey.

For his morning tea
A priest sits down
In utter silence –
Confronted by chrysanthemums.

> With your singing
> Make me lonelier than ever,
> You, solitary bird,
> Cuckoo of the forest.

> A white narcissus
> And a white paper screen
> Illuminate each other
> In this quiet room.

Now, taken at the surface level, all these poems are purely descriptive, but if one broods upon these poems long enough, one realizes that they also have a symbolic quality. This symbolic quality inherent in the poem is called by Bashō *sabi* (loneliness), *shiori* (tenderness), and *hosomi* (slenderness), depending on the mode of its manifestation and the degree of its saturation. Although definition of these terms in any strict manner would only lead to misunderstanding, let us take, for example, what Bashō says (through the mouth of a disciple[23]) about *sabi*.

Sabi is in the colour of a poem. It does not necessarily refer to the poem that describes a lonely scene. If a man goes to war wearing a stout armour or to a party dressed up in gay clothes, and if this man happens to be an old man, there is something lonely about him. *Sabi* is something like that. It is in the poem regardless of the scene it describes – whether it is lonely or gay. In the following poem, for example, I find a great deal of *sabi*.

> Under the cherry
> Flower guards have assembled
> To chatter –
> Their hoary heads together.

In other words, *sabi* is the subjective element, deeply buried in the objective element of the poem, but giving it a profound wealth of symbolic meaning. It is indeed by these qualities of *sabi*, *shiori*, and *hosomi* that Bashō's mature style is distinguished from the styles of his predecessors or his own immature style.

It is necessary, I believe, for us to turn at this point to the special features of Bashō's linking technique. I have already pointed out that Teitoku's linking technique was based on verbal association (*mono-zuke*) and Sōin's on clever interpretation and ingenious transfer (*kokoro-zuke*). Bashō says that in his case the link is provided by what he calls the aroma (*nioi*), echo (*hibiki*), countenance (*omokage*), colour (*utsuri*) and rank (*kurai*) of the preceding poem. Here again the strict definition of the individual terms would only cause confusion, but let us take as an example what Bashō (again through the mouth of a disciple[24]) says about *hibiki*.

When you hit something, the noise comes back to you in a matter of an instant. This is what I mean by *hibiki*. In the following pair, for example, the second poem is a perfect echo of the first.

> Against the wooden floor
> I threw a silver-glazed cup
> Breaking it to pieces.

> Look, now, the slender curve
> Of your sword, half-drawn.

Even through this brief explanation, I think it is clear that the special features of Bashō's linking technique exist in its imaginative quality. Instead of lashing the poems together forcibly by wit or ingenuity, Bashō moors them, so to speak, with a fine thread of imaginative harmony, giving each poem fair play. It is indeed by virtue of this imaginative linking technique (*nioi-zuke*) that Bashō was able to achieve

an unprecedented degree of perfection in his linked verse.
Let me quote here the first few poems of a linked verse
collected in *Saru Mino* as an example of his superb effect.

> Combed in neat order
> By the first shower
> Of winter –
> Thick plumage of a kite.
>
> A storm having passed, fallen leaves
> Have settled themselves on the ground.
>
> Early in the morning
> I wade across the swollen river
> My trousers in water.
>
> Silent air is broken by farmers ringing
> Piercing alarms to drive a badger away.
>
> In twilight, the horned moon
> Reaches to the ruined lattice-door
> Through an overgrown ivy.
>
> Here is a greedy man who keeps to himself
> The beautiful pears ripe in his garden.[25]

Here is indeed something that is comparable to Sōgi's
masterpiece in seriousness and elegance, and to the best of
Sōin's poems in freedom and energy.

Bashō returned to Edo from his third major journey after
two and a half years of wandering, in the winter of 1691,
and in the spring of the following year a new house was
built for him. Bashō spent the next two and a half years in
this house. For a number of reasons, however, Bashō's life
of this period was not a happy one. An unusual degree of

ennui is expressed in the essay he wrote in 1693 to announce his determination to live in complete isolation.

If someone comes to see me, I have to waste my words in vain. If I leave my house to visit others, I waste their time in vain. Following the examples of Sonkei and Togorō, therefore, I have decided to live in complete isolation with a firmly closed door. My solitude shall be my company, and my poverty my wealth. Already a man of fifty, I should be able to maintain this self-imposed discipline.

> Only for morning glories
> I open my door –
> During the daytime I keep it
> Tightly barred.

Two anthologies of importance were the product of these two and a half years in Edo. They are *Fukagawa Shū* (*Fukagawa Anthology*) and *Sumidawara* (*A Charcoal Sack*), the latter being the sixth of the *Major Anthologies*. In the poems Bashō wrote during this period, however, there was a strange sense of detachment from life, which sometimes produced a slightly comical effect – what Bashō called *karumi* (lightness), but at other times a somewhat sombre effect. For example,

> A bush-warbler,
> Coming to the verandah-edge,
> Left its droppings
> On the rice-cakes.

> The wild cries of a cat
> Having been hushed,
> The soft beams of the moon
> Touched my bedroom.

Warming myself
At an ashy fire,
I saw on the wall
The shadow of my guest.

The voice of a cuckoo
Dropped to the lake
Where it lay floating
On the surface.

Confined by winter,
A man is guarded
By an age-old pine
On the golden screen.

In audacious quickness
The spring sun rose
Over a mountain-path,
Sweet scent of the plum.

In the sky
Of eight or nine yards
Above the willow –
Drizzling rain.

In the spring of 1694, Bashō left on the last of his major journeys. This time he was determined to travel, if possible, to the southern end of Japan. He was already fifty, however, and his health was failing. The poems he wrote on this journey suggest something almost like a shadow of death. For example,

Autumn drawing near,
My heart of itself
Inclines to a cosy room
Of four-and-a-half mats.

My feet against
A cold plastered wall,
I took a midday nap
Late in summer.

Ancient city of Nara,
Ancient images of Buddha,
Shrouded in the scent
Of Chrysanthemums.

Deep is autumn,
And in its deep air
I somehow wondered
Who my neighbour is.

While Bashō was lingering in Ōsaka and its vicinity, he fell
a victim to what seems to have been an attack of dysentery.
Here is a vivid description of his condition four days before
his death by one of his disciples.[26]

On the night of October the eighth, though it was almost mid-
night, Donshū was summoned to our master's bedside. Soon I
heard the clatter of an ink bar rubbing against a slab. I wondered
what manner of letter it was, but it turned out to be a poem. It
was entitled, 'Sick in bed'.

Seized with a disease
Halfway on the road,
My dreams keep revolving
Round the withered moor.

Later I was summoned by our master, who told me that he had
in mind another poem which ended like this:

Round, as yet round,
My dreams keep revolving.

And he asked me which one I preferred. I wanted to know what
preceded these lines, of course, but thinking that my question

47

would merely give him discomfort, I said I preferred the first one. Now it is a matter of deep regret that I did not put the question to him, for there is no way of knowing what a beautiful poem the second was.

Thus died on 12 October 1694 one of the greatest geniuses in Japanese literature, and five years after his death, the last of his *Major Anthologies, Zoku Saru Mino* (*A Coat for a Monkey, Continued*), was published, being the collection of the poems he wrote in the last few years. Fortunately, however, his works survived him, and through them we can enter into the inner depths of this great man. His travel sketches, in particular, show him at his best or on his way to his best, for they are, as I have already pointed out, the products of his ripest years. Now the reader is invited to read them in an English translation.

One final comment on the technique of translation. I have used a four-line stanza in translating *haiku* just as I did in my former translation (*The Year of My Life*, a translation of Issa's *Oraga Haru*, University of California Press). I shall not, of course, try to defend my stanza, for it is an experiment, and just as any other experiment in literature, the result alone can justify or disqualify it. Let me, however, state here at least three reasons for my choice. First, the language of *haiku*, as I have already pointed out, is based on colloquialism, and in my opinion, the closest approximation of natural conversational rhythm can be achieved in English by a four-line stanza rather than a constrained three-line stanza. Second, even in the lifetime of Bashō, *hokku* (the starting piece of a linked verse) was given a special place in the series and treated half-independently, and in my opinion, a three-line stanza does not carry adequate dignity and weight to compare with *hokku*. Finally, I had before me the task of translating a great number of poems mixed with prose, and I found it impossible to use three-line form consistently. In any case, this translation is primarily intended for lovers of poetry, and only secondarily for scholars whose minds should be broad enough to recognize the use in a translation like this. The present translation is not for those purists who insist (without believing either in its validity or possibility, I presume) that *haiku* should be translated with the original seventeen syllable scheme or at least into three lines.

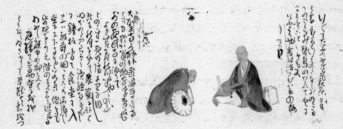

The illustrations in the text are by Buson, who is counted not only among the three best *haiku* poets of Japan but also among the outstanding painters of his day. By way of concluding my introduction, let me quote the inscription and poem from the portrait of Bashō by Buson[27] used for the cover.

> Neither speak ill of others, nor well of yourself.
> > The moment you open
> > Your mouth to speak,
> > The autumn wind stirs
> > And chills your lips.

THE RECORDS OF A
WEATHER-EXPOSED SKELETON

FOLLOWING the example of the ancient priest[1] who is said to have travelled thousands of miles caring naught for his provisions and attaining the state of sheer ecstasy under the pure beams of the moon, I left my broken house on the River Sumida in the August of the first year of Jyōkyō[2] among the wails of the autumn wind.

> Determined to fall
> A weather-exposed skeleton
> I cannot help the sore wind
> Blowing through my heart.

> After ten autumns
> In Edo, my mind
> Points back to it
> As my native place.

I crossed the barrier-gate of Hakone on a rainy day. All the mountains were deeply buried behind the clouds.

> In a way
> It was fun
> Not to see Mount Fuji
> In foggy rain.

On this journey, I am accompanied by a young man named Chiri,[3] who kindly assumes the position of a servant and renders what help he can for my benefit along the way.

He is a man of true affection, and trustworthy enough to be called a friend in need.

> I left my master's house
> In Fukagawa,
> Leaving its Bashō tree
> In the care of Mount Fuji.   *Written by Chiri*

As I was plodding along the River Fuji, I saw a small child, hardly three years of age, crying pitifully on the bank, obviously abandoned by his parents. They must have thought this child was unable to ride through the stormy waters of life which run as wild as the rapid river itself, and that he was destined to have a life even shorter than that of the morning dew. The child looked to me as fragile as the flowers of bush-clover that scatter at the slightest stir of the autumn wind, and it was so pitiful that I gave him what little food I had with me.

> The ancient poet
> Who pitied monkeys for their cries,
> What would he say, if he saw
> This child crying in the autumn wind?[4]

How is it indeed that this child has been reduced to this state of utter misery? Is it because of his mother who ignored him, or because of his father who abandoned him? Alas, it seems to me that this child's undeserved suffering has been caused by something far greater and more massive – by what one might call the irresistible will of heaven. If it is so, child, you must raise your voice to heaven, and I must pass on, leaving you behind.

The day I wanted to cross the River Ōi, it rained from morning till night, and I was held up by the swollen river.

> A long rainy day of autumn,
> My friends in Edo
> Are perhaps counting the days,
> Thinking of us at the River Ōi.[5]

Written by Chiri

A scene before my eyes:

> Roses of Sharon
> At the roadside
> Perishing one after another
> In the mouth of a horse.

I travelled a few miles on horseback, half-asleep, with my whip swinging by my side, exactly in the manner of the Chinese Poet, Toboku.[6] There was an aged moon faintly hanging in the sky while the foot of the mountains was dark as a hollow. It was a bit too early even for the first cock-crow, but my dreams were suddenly interrupted when my horse came to the steep precipice of Sayo-no-nakayama.

> Half-asleep on horseback
> I saw as if in a dream
> A distant moon and a line of smoke
> For the morning tea.

I went down to Ise where I spent ten days with a friend named Fūbaku.[7] I visited the outer shrine of Ise one evening just before dark. The first gate of the shrine was standing in the shadow, and the lights were glimmering in the background. As I stood there, lending my ears to the roar of pine trees upon distant mountains, I felt moved deep in the bottom of my heart.

> In the utter darkness
> Of a moonless night,
> A powerful wind embraces
> The ancient cedar trees.[8]

I do not wear a single piece of metal on my belt, nor do I carry anything but a sack on my shoulder. My head is clean shaven, and I have a string of beads in my hand. I am indeed dressed like a priest, but priest I am not, for the dust of the world still clings to me. The keeper of the inner shrine prevented me from entering the holy seat of the god because my appearance was like a Buddhist priest.

At the bottom of the valley where the ancient Poet, Saigyō,[9] is said to have erected his hermitage, there was a stream and a woman was washing potatoes.

> The Poet Saigyō
> Would have written a poem
> Even for the woman
> Washing potatoes.[10]

Towards the end of the day I stopped at a small tea house, where a young woman named Butterfly handed me a small piece of white silk and asked me to write a poem choosing her name as the subject.

> A Butterfly
> Poised on a tender orchid,
> How sweetly the incense
> Burns on its wings.

I visited a poet at his hermitage.

> An ivy spray
> Trained up over the wall
> And a few bamboos
> Inviting a tempest.

At last I reached my native village in the beginning of September, but I could not find a single trace of the herbs my mother used to grow in front of her room. The herbs must have been completely bitten away by the frost. Nothing remained the same in my native village. Even the faces of my brothers had changed with wrinkles and white hair, and we simply rejoiced to see each other alive. My eldest brother took out a small amulet bag, and said to me as he opened it, 'See your mother's frosty hairs. You are like Urashima[11] whose hair was turned white upon his opening a miracle box.' After remaining in tears for a few moments, I wrote:

> Should I hold them in my hand,
> They will disappear
> In the warmth of my tears,
> Icy strings of frost.[12]

Crossing over to the country of Yamato, we came to a village called Takenouchi in the province of Katsuge. This is where my companion Chiri was born. We spent several days resting our tired feet.

There was a house deeply buried in a bamboo thicket.

> Sweet as a lute
> Falls on my ears,

The plucking of a cotton bow
In a dark bamboo recess.

I saw a huge pine tree, probably over a thousand years old, in the garden of the Taima Temple at the foot of Mount Futagami. The trunk was large enough to hold a bull. As I stood in front of this tree, I felt a strange sense of awe and respect, for, though the tree itself was a cold senseless object, it had survived the punishment of an axe for so many years under the divine protection of Buddha.

How many priests
How many morning glories
Have perished under the pine
Eternal as law?

I wandered all by myself into the heart of the mountains of Yoshino. White masses of clouds were piled up over the peaks, and all the valleys were filled with smoky rain. Tiny houses of woodcutters were scattered along the mountain sides, and the sound of an axe on the western slope was echoed by the mountains on the east. The bells from various temples struck deep to the innermost part of my being. Many ancient poets had chosen to live among these mountains, completely isolated from the rest of the world. It was only natural for them to compare these mountains with Mount Rozan[13] in China.

I lodged at an annex of a certain temple. In the utter silence of the night I wrote:

Beat your fulling block,
And let me at least

Hear its sound,
My dear temple wife.[14]

The grassy hermitage of Saigyō was about two hundred yards behind the innermost temple of Yoshino. It was separated by a steep valley and approachable only by a narrow trail covered with leaves. The famed spring was just as it had been when the poet described it, shedding its clear drops of water with a drip-drop sound.

I like to wash,
By way of experiment,
The dust of this world
In the droplets of dew.[15]

If Hakui[16] had escaped from his wicked king and come to Japan, he would have certainly cleansed his mouth with the water of this spring, and similarly, if Kyoyū[17] had heard about this spring, he would have come all the way to wash his defiled ears. When I finally decided to descend the mountain, the late afternoon sun of autumn was pouring its almost level light, so I skipped all other famous places and went directly to the mausoleum of Emperor Godaigo.[18]

The weedy grass
Called reminiscence
Reminiscent of the bygone days
In front of the Mausoleum.[19]

I travelled through the provinces of Yamato and Yamashiro, and entered the province of Mino by way of Ōmi. Passing through the mountainous villages of Imasu and

Yamanaka, I went to see the tomb of Lady Tokiwa,[20] the ill-fated mistress of the wicked Lord Yoshitomo.[21] Moritake,[22] a keeper of the Ise Shrine, must have seen a resemblance between Lord Yoshitomo and the cold wind raging around the tomb when he compared the two in one of his poems. I, too, wrote:

> The autumn wind,
> Resembling somewhat
> The frozen heart
> Of Lord Yoshitomo.

I visited the barrier-gate of Fuwa.

> Thickets, fields,
> And all else that is,
> Were once the gate of Fuwa –
> The autumn wind blows.

I spent a night in Ōgaki as a guest of the Poet Bokuin.[23] Indeed I have come a long way since I left my house in Musashino, determined to become a weather-exposed skeleton.

> Still alive I am
> At the end of a long dream
> On my journey,
> Fall of an autumn day.

I visited the Hontō Temple in Kuwana.

> Mid-winter peonies
> And a distant plover singing,
> Did I hear a cuckoo
> In the snow?

Tired of sleeping on a grass pillow, I went down to the seashore before break of day.

> Early dawn,
> Young white fish
> Shining in ephemeral white,
> Hardly an inch long.

I went to see the Atsuta Shrine, but it had been reduced to utter ruins. Walls had crumbled and dry grasses were standing among the fallen blocks. There were ropes, here and there, showing the sites of the extinct shrines, and stones engraved with the names of the gods once enshrined therein. A shock of brown sage-brush and overgrown 'reminiscence' gave me an impression not altogether pleasing but strangely lasting.

> Even the weedy reminiscences
> Are dead,
> I bought and ate
> Some rice-cake at an inn.

On my way through Nagoya, where crazy Chikusai[24] is said to have practised quackery and poetry, I wrote:

> With a bit of madness in me,
> Which is poetry,
> I plod along like Chikusai
> Among the wails of the wind.[25]

> Sleeping on a grass pillow
> I hear now and then
> The nocturnal bark of a dog
> In the passing rain.

I went to a snow-viewing party.

> Gladly will I sell
> For profit,
> Dear merchants of the town,
> My hat laden with snow.

I saw a traveller on my way.

> Even a horse
> Is a spectacle,
> I cannot help stopping to see it
> On the morning of snow.

I spent the whole afternoon at the beach.

> Over the darkened sea,
> Only the voice of a flying duck
> Is visible –
> In soft white.[26]

The end of the year came, while I was thus travelling here and there.

> With a hat on my head
> And straw sandals on my feet,
> I met on the road
> The end of the year.

Yet I reached my house in my native village in time to welcome the new year.

> Whose bridegroom may it be?
> I see a cow
> Loaded with rice-cake and green fern
> In the year of the cow.

On my way to Nara, I wrote:

> It is spring,
> Even nameless hills
> Are decorated
> With thin films of morning mist.

I visited the Nigatsudō Temple, at the time of its ceremony.

> Water-drawing ceremony,[27]
> The wooden clogs of the priests
> Beat against
> The icy floor of the hall.

I went up to Kyōto, where I visited Mitsui Shūfū[28] at his house by the Narutaki waterfall. There was a plum orchard.

> Blanket of white plum,
> I wonder what happened to the cranes,
> Stolen or hidden
> Behind the plum blossoms?

> A sturdy oak
> In the plum orchard,
> Totally indifferent
> To the blossoms.

I visited the Priest Ninkō[29] at Saiganji Temple in the village of Fushimi.

> Shed your tears of joy
> On my sleeves,
> Peach blossoms of Fushimi,
> On this day of reunion.

I crossed a mountain on my way to Ōtsu.

> I picked my way
> Through a mountain road,
> And I was greeted
> By a smiling violet.

A distant view of Lake Biwa:

> Far and distant,
> Lighter than cherry blossoms,
> Floating like a mirage,
> The pine tree of Karasaki.

I stopped at a certain shop for lunch.

> A branch of wild azalea
> Thrown into a bucket,
> Behind, a woman tearing
> The meat of a dried codfish.[30]

A roadside scene:

> Wild sparrows
> In a patch of yellow rape,
> Pretending to admire
> The flowers.

I met an old friend of mine[31] at Minakuchi, after twenty years of separation.

> A lively cherry
> In full bloom
> Between the two lives
> Now made one.

A priest from Hiru-ga-kojima in the country of Izu, who had been travelling by himself since the autumn of the previous year, heard about me and wanted to enjoy my company. He followed me all the way into the country of Owari, where he finally caught up with me.

> Together let us eat
> Ears of wheat,
> Sharing at night
> A grass pillow.

This priest told me that Daiten,[32] the chief priest of the Engakuji Temple, had died this January. It was such a surprise that I could hardly believe my ears. I wrote a quick letter to Kikaku,[33] relating the news.

> Reminiscent of the plum
> Scattered beyond recall,
> I pay homage to a white *unohana*
> With my tearful eyes.

A poem given to Tokoku:[34]

> Fluttering butterfly
> On a white poppy,
> He would wrest his wings
> For a token of love.

I stopped again at the house of my friend, Tōyō,[35] on my way home. I left the following poem at the time of my departure from his house, bound for the eastern provinces.

> Having sucked deep
> In a sweet peony,

A bee creeps
Out of its hairy recesses.[36]

On my way through the country of Kai, I stopped at an isolated inn in the mountains.

What a luxury it is
For a travelling horse
To feed on the wheat
At a hospitable inn!

I reached home at long last towards the end of April. After several days of rest, I wrote:

Shed of everything else,
I still have some lice
I picked up on the road –
Crawling on my summer robes.

A VISIT TO
THE KASHIMA SHRINE

VISITING the Suma Beach on the night of the autumnal full moon, Teishitsu,[1] a poet from Kyōto, is said to have written,

> Crouching under a pine
> I watched the full moon,
> Pondering all night long
> On the sorrow of Chūnagon.[2]

Having for some time cherished in my mind the memory of this poet, I wandered out on to the road at last one day this past autumn, possessed by an irresistible desire to see the rise of the full moon over the mountains of the Kashima Shrine. I was accompanied by two men. One was a masterless youth and the other was a wandering priest. The latter was clad in a robe black as a crow, with a bundle of sacred stoles around his neck and on his back a portable shrine containing a holy image of the Buddha-after-enlightenment. This priest, brandishing his long staff, stepped into the road, ahead of all the others, as if he had a free pass to the World beyond the Gateless Gate. I, too, was clad in a black robe, but neither a priest nor an ordinary man of this world was I, for I wavered ceaselessly like a bat that passes for a bird at one time and for a mouse at another. We got on a boat near my house and sailed to the town of Gyōtoku, where, landing from our boat, we proceeded without hiring a horse, for we wanted to try the strength of our slender legs.

Covering our heads with cypress hats, which were a kind gift of a certain friend in the province of Kai, we walked along, till, having passed the village of Yahata we came to the endless grass-moor called Kamagai-no-hara. In China, it is said, there is a wide field where one can command a distance of one thousand miles by a single glance, but here our eyes swept over the grass unobstructed, till finally they rested upon the twin peaks of Mount Tsukuba soaring above the horizon. Rising into heaven, like two swords piercing the sky, these peaks vie with the famous twin peaks of Mount Rozan in China.[3]

> Not to mention
> The beauty of its snow,
> Mount Tsukuba shines forth
> In its purple robes.

This is a poem written by Ransetsu,[4] my disciple, upon his visit here. Prince Yamatotakeru[5] also immortalized this mountain in his poem, and the first anthology of linked verse[6] was named after this mountain. Indeed such is the beauty of the mountain that few poets have found it possible to pass by it without composing a poem of their own, be it *waka* or *haiku*.

Scattered all around me were the flowers of bush-clover. As I watched them in amazement, I could not help admiring Tamenaka[7] who is said to have carried sprays of bush-clover in his luggage all the way to Kyōto as a souvenir. Among the bush-clover were other wild flowers in bloom, such as bellflower, valerian, pampas large and small, all tangled in great confusion. The belling of wild stags, probably calling their mates, was heard now and then, and herds of horses were seen stepping proudly as they trampled upon the grass.

We reached the town of Fusa on the banks of the River Tone towards nightfall. The fishermen of this town catch salmon by spreading wickerwork traps in the river, and sell it in the markets in Edo. We went into one of the fishermen's huts and had a short sleep amidst the fishy smell. Upon waking, however, we hired a boat, and, descending the river under the bright beams of the moon, arrived at the Kashima Shrine.

On the following day it started to rain in the afternoon, and in no way could we see the rise of the full moon. I was told that the former priest of the Komponji Temple was living in seclusion at the foot of the hill where the shrine was situated. So I went to see him, and was granted a night's shelter. The tranquillity of the priest's hermitage was such that it inspired, in the words of an ancient poet, 'a profound sense of meditation' in my heart, and for a while at least I was able to forget the fretful feeling I had about not being able to see the full moon. Shortly before daybreak, however, the moon began to shine through the rifts made in the hanging clouds. I immediately wakened the priest, and other members of the household followed him out of bed. We sat for a long time in utter silence, watching the moonlight trying to penetrate the clouds and listening to the sound of the lingering rain. It was really regrettable that I had come such a long way only to look at the dark shadow of the moon, but I consoled myself by remembering the famous lady who had returned without composing a single poem from the long walk she had taken to hear a cuckoo.[8] The following are the poems we composed on this occasion:

> Regardless of weather,
> The moon shines the same;
> It is the drifting clouds
> That make it seem different
> On different nights.   *Written by the priest*

> Swift the moon
> Across the sky,
> Treetops below
> Dripping with rain.   *Written by Tōsei*[9]

> Having slept
> In a temple,
> I watched the moon
> With a solemn look.   *Written by Tōsei*

> Having slept
> In the rain,
> The bamboo corrected itself
> To view the moon.   *Written by Sora*[10]

> How lonely it is
> To look at the moon
> Hearing in a temple
> Eavesdrops pattering.   *Written by Sōha*[11]

Poems composed at the Kashima Shrine:

> In the days
> Of the ancient gods,
> A mere seedling
> This pine must have been.   *Written by Tōsei*

A Visit to the Kashima Shrine

Let us wipe
In solemn penitence
Dew-drops gathered
On the sacred stone.   *Written by Sōha*

In front of the shrine
Even stags kneel down
To worship,
Raising pitiful cries.   *Written by Sora*

Poems composed at a farm-house:

A solitary crane
In the half-reaped paddies,
The autumn deepens
In the village.   *Written by Tōsei*

Under this bright moon
Over the village,
Let me help the farmers
Harvest rice.   *Written by Sōha*

A farmer's child
Hulling rice
Arrests his hands
To look at the moon.   *Written by Tōsei*

Potato leaves
On incinerated ground,
I awaited tiptoe
The rise of the moon.   *Written by Tōsei*

Bashō

Poems composed in a field:

> Dyed a gay colour
> My trousers will be
> By the bush-clovers
> In full bloom.   *Written by Sora*

> In mid-autumn
> Horses are left to graze
> Till they fall replete
> In the flowering grass.   *Written by Sora*

> Bush clovers,
> Be kind enough to take in
> This pack of mountain dogs
> At least for a night.   *Written by Tōsei*

Poems composed at Jijun's[12] house where we stopped on our way home:

> Friend sparrows,
> Sleep, if you please,
> Haystack-enclosed
> At my house.   *Written by the host*

> Surrounded by a thick foliage of cedars,
> Your house stands, pregnant with autumn.
>   *Written by the guest*

> We started out
> On our moon-viewing trip,
> Calling to halt
> A boat ascending the river.   *Written by Sora*

The twenty-fifth of August, the Fourth Year of Jyōkyō.[13]

THE RECORDS OF A
TRAVEL-WORN SATCHEL

In this mortal frame of mine which is made of a hundred bones and nine orifices there is something, and this something is called a wind-swept spirit for lack of a better name, for it is much like a thin drapery that is torn and swept away at the slighest stir of the wind. This something in me took to writing poetry years ago, merely to amuse itself at first, but finally making it its lifelong business. It must be admitted, however, that there were times when it sank into such dejection that it was almost ready to drop its pursuit, or again times when it was so puffed up with pride that it exulted in vain victories over the others. Indeed, ever since it began to write poetry, it has never found peace with itself, always wavering between doubts of one kind and another. At one time it wanted to gain security by entering the service of a court, and at another it wished to measure the depth of its ignorance by trying to be a scholar, but it was prevented from either because of its unquenchable love of poetry. The fact is, it knows no other art than the art of writing poetry, and therefore, it hangs on to it more or less blindly.

Saigyō[1] in traditional poetry, Sōgi[2] in linked verse, Sesshū[3] in painting, Rikyū[4] in tea ceremony, and indeed all who have achieved real excellence in any art, possess one thing in common, that is, a mind to obey nature, to be one with nature, throughout the four seasons of the year.

Whatever such a mind sees is a flower, and whatever such a mind dreams of is the moon. It is only a barbarous mind that sees other than the flower, merely an animal mind that dreams of other than the moon. The first lesson for the artist is, therefore, to learn how to overcome such barbarism and animality, to follow nature, to be one with nature.

It was early in October when the sky was terribly uncertain that I decided to set out on a journey. I could not help feeling vague misgivings about the future of my journey, as I watched the fallen leaves of autumn being carried away by the wind.

> From this day forth
> I shall be called a wanderer,
> Leaving on a journey
> Thus among the early showers.

> You will again sleep night after night
> Nestled among the flowers of sasanqua.[5]

The second of these poems was written to encourage me by Chōtarō,[6] a native of Iwaki, when he held a farewell party for me at the house of Kikaku.[7]

> It is winter now,
> But when the spring comes,
> Your bundle shall contain
> Cherry-blossoms of Yoshino.

This poem was an extremely courteous gift of Lord Rosen.[8] Other friends, relatives and students of mine followed his example by visiting me with poems and letters of farewell or sending me money for straw sandals, so that

I was spared the trouble of preparing for my journey, which normally, it is said, takes as long as three months. In fact, everything I needed for my journey – the paper raincoat, the cotton-stuffed mantle, the hat, the stockings, etc, to keep me warm in the dead of winter – was given me by my friends, and as I was invited to parties on a boat, at my friends' houses, or even at my own hermitage, I became used to the pomp and splendour of feasting unawares and almost fell a victim to the illusion that a man of importance was leaving on a journey.

From time immemorial the art of keeping diaries while on the road was popular among the people, and such great writers as Lord Ki,[9] Chōmei,[10] and the nun Abutsu[11] brought it to perfection. Later works are by and large little more than imitations of these great masters, and my pen, being weak in wisdom and unfavoured by divine gift, strives to equal them, but in vain. It is easy enough to say, for example, that such and such a day was rainy in the morning but fine in the afternoon, that there was a pine tree at such and such a place, or that the name of the river at a certain place was such and such, for these things are what everybody says in their diaries, although in fact they are not even worth mentioning unless there are fresh and arresting elements in them. The readers will find in my diary a random collection of what I have seen on the road, views somehow remaining in my heart – an isolated house in the mountains, or a lonely inn surrounded by the moor, for example. I jotted down these records with the hope that they might provoke pleasant conversation among my readers and that they might be of some use to those who would travel the same way. Nevertheless, I must admit that

my records are little more than the babble of the intoxi-
cated and the rambling talk of the dreaming, and therefore
my readers are kindly requested to take them as such.

I stopped overnight at Narumi.

> The voices of plovers
> Invite me to stare
> Into the darkness
> O f the Starlit Promontory.[12]

The host of the inn told me that Lord Asukai Masaaki[13]
had once lodged here on his way from Kyōto and left be-
hind him the following poem in his own handwriting.

> As I stand alone
> On the beach of Narumi,
> I feel the expanse of the sea
> That severs me so
> From the ancient capital.

I myself wrote:

> Only half the way I came
> To the ancient capital,
> And above my head
> Clouds heavy with snow.

I wanted to visit Tokoku[14] at his hermitage in the village
of Hobi in the province of Mikawa. I first sent for Etsujin,[15]
and we walked together twenty-five miles or so in the
direction of the village till we put up at an inn at Yoshida.

> Cold as it was,
> We felt secure
> Sleeping together
> In the same room.

I followed a narrow winding path in the middle of rice fields at Amatsu Nawate among the biting blasts from the sea.

> In the sun
> Of a cold winter day,
> My shadow had frozen stiff
> On horseback.

The promontory of Irago was about a mile from the village of Hobi. One could reach it by land from the province of Mikawa, but from the province of Ise one had to cross the ocean, and yet it was somehow included among the sights of Ise by a poet of *Manyō Shū*.[16] I picked some pebbles on the beach, the so-called white stones of Irago used for the games of *go*.[17] Mount Honeyama behind was famous for hawks, for this southern promontory was one of the places where hawks came very early each year. Just as I was trying to recall ancient poems on the hawk,

> By a singular stroke
> Of luck, I saw
> A solitary hawk circling
> Above the promontory of Irago.

The Atsuta Shrine was under reconstruction.

> Not a flaw there is
> On the polished surface
> Of the divine glass,
> Chaste with flowers of snow.

I was invited to Nagoya, a city to the west of the Atsuta Shrine, to have a short rest.

Surely there must be
Someone crossing
The pass of Hakone
On this snowy morning.

I was invited to a party.

Stretching by force
The wrinkles of my coat,
I started out on a walk
To a snow-viewing party.

Deep as the snow is,
Let me go as far as I can
Till I stumble and fall,
Viewing the white landscape.

I was a guest poet at my friend's house.

Searching for the scent
Of the early plum,
I found it by the eaves
Of a proud storehouse.

During my stay in Nagoya, I composed quite a number
of linked verses, long and short, with my friends who had
come from Ōgaki and Gifu.

I left Nagoya, however, several days after December the
tenth, headed for my native place.

Spending an idle day
At an inn, I saw people

Dusting their houses
At the end of the year.

At the village of Hinaga, where it is said an ancient poet[18]
coming from Kuwana found himself almost starved to
death, I hired a horse and climbed the steep slope of the
Support-yourself-on-a-stick Pass.[19] As I was unaccustomed
to horse-riding, however, I had a fall at one point, the
saddle and myself overthrown by a jerk.

Had I crossed the pass
Supported by a stick,
I would have spared myself
The fall from the horse.

Out of the depressing feeling that accompanied the fall, I
wrote the above poem impromptu, but found it devoid of
the seasonal word.

Coming home at last
At the end of the year,
I wept to find
My old umbilical cord.

Unwilling to part with the passing year, I drank till late
on the last day of December. When I awoke after a long
sleep, the first day of the new year was more than half gone.

On the second at least
I will get up early
To give welcome
To the floral spring.

Scenes of early spring:

> Fresh spring!
> The world is only
> Nine days old –
> These fields and mountains!

> Heated spring air
> In tiny waves
> Of an inch or two –
> Above wintery grass.

There was the ruined site of the temple built by the high priest Shunjō[20] at the village of Awa in the province of Iga. The name of this temple was known to have been Gohōzan Shindaibutsuji, but now this long name alone was the witness of its past glory. The main hall had been completely destroyed, leaving only foundations, and the priests' living quarters had been reduced to paddies and fields. The tall statue of Buddha, originally six feet and six inches tall, had become covered with green moss save for the divine face that shone forth as in former days. The image of the founder stood erect, but it was a pity to see it among the ruins, where sage-brush and other weeds had grown rank on empty stone platforms and pedestals. Dead, too, were the couple of sacred *sal* trees that had once been the pride of the temple.

> Almost as high
> As the crumbled statue,
> The heated air shimmering
> From the stone foundation.

> Many things of the past
> Are brought to my mind,
> As I stand in the garden
> Staring at a cherry tree.

I paid a visit to the shrine at Ise Yamada.

> Not knowing
> The name of the tree,
> I stood in the flood
> Of its sweet smell.

> It is a bit too cold
> To be naked
> In this stormy wind
> Of February.

At Bodaisan:

> Tell me the loneliness
> Of this deserted mountain,
> The aged farmer
> Digging wild potatoes.

Upon meeting my friend, Ryū Shōsha.[21]

> 'Before all else tell me
> The name of this rush,'
> I said to the scholar,
> Pointing to the young leaves.

I met Setsudō, son of Ajiro Minbu.[22]

> A young shoot has borne
> Beautiful flowers,

Growing upon
An aged plum tree.

I was invited to a hermitage.

Surrounded by potato fields,
The gate stands,
Half buried by the fresh leaves
Of goose grass.

I wondered why there was not a single plum tree in the holy compound of the Ise Shrine. The priest, however, told me that there was no special reason, and that I could find a solitary stock in the back of the house where the sacred virgins lived.

How befitting it is
For holy virgins,
A solitary stock of
Fragrant plum.

What a stroke of luck
It is to see
A picture of Nirvana
In this holy compound!

When the middle of March came, I could no longer suppress the desire to leave for Yoshino, for in my mind the cherry blossoms were already in full bloom. There was a man who promised to accompany me to Yoshino at the promontory of Irago, and he joined me at Ise.[23] He was eager to enjoy various views with me and also to help me as a servant while on the road. He changed his name to Mangiku-maru, which I liked exceedingly for its boyish flavour. We celebrated our start by scribbling on our hats 'Nowhere in this wide universe have we a fixed abode – A party of two wanderers'.

> Wait a while,
> I will show you
> The cherries of Yoshino,
> My cypress hat.

> Wait a while,
> My cypress hat,
> I will show you too
> The cherries of Yoshino.
>
> *Written by Mangiku-maru*

I threw away quite a number of things, for I believed in travelling light. There were certain things, however, I had to carry on my back – such as a raincoat, an overcoat, an inkstone, a brush, writing paper, medicine, a lunch basket – and these constituted quite a load for me. I made such slow progress that I felt deeply depressed as I walked along with faltering steps, giving as much power as I could to my trembling knees.

> Tired of walking
> I put up at an inn,
> Embraced comfortably
> By wisteria flowers.

Bashō

At Hatsuse:

> There is a man
> Sitting for meditation
> In a temple corner
> On a spring night.

> Priests are walking
> In high clogs
> Among the rain that falls
> On cherry blossoms.   *Written by Mangiku*

At Mount Kazuraki:

> God of this mountain,
> May you be kind enough
> To show me your face
> Among the dawning blossoms?

After visits to Mount Miwa and Mount Tafu, I climbed
the steep pass of Hoso.

> Higher than the lark
> I climbed into the air,
> Taking breath
> At the summit of a pass.

At the waterfall called Dragon's Gate:[24]

> A spray of blossoms
> On the Dragon's Gate
> Would be an excellent gift
> For tipplers.

Tipplers would be overjoyed
To hear from me
About this bridge of blossoms
Across the waterfall.

At Nijikkō:

> One after another
> In silent succession fall
> The flowers of yellow rose –
> The roar of tumbling water.

I visited the waterfalls of Seirei, Furu, Nunobiki, and Minō, the second being slightly less than half a mile from the shrine of Furu, and the last on the way to the temple of Kachio.

Cherry blossoms:

> From five to six miles
> I walk every day
> In search of you,
> Cherry blossoms.

> Cherry blossoms
> In the darkening sky,
> And among them a melancholy
> Ready-to-bloom-tomorrow.[25]

> Using my fan
> For a cup,
> I pretended to drink
> Under the scattering cherry.

Upon seeing a crystal spring coming out of a mossy rock:

> The spring rain
> Must have penetrated
> Through the leaves
> To feed the crystal spring.

During my three days' stay in Yoshino, I had a chance to see the cherry blossoms at different hours of the day – at early dawn, late in the evening, or past midnight when the dying moon was in the sky. Overwhelmed by the scenes, however, I was not able to compose a single poem. My heart was heavy, for I remembered the famous poems of Sesshōkō,[26] Saigyō, Teishitsu and other ancient poets. In spite of the ambitiousness of my original purpose, I thus found the present journey utterly devoid of poetic success.

At Mount Kōya:

> Hearing a pheasant
> In the mountains,
> I pine with the warmest love
> For my father and mother.

> Because of my hair
> I suffered a humiliation
> Under the scattering cherry
> At the holiest of shrines.

> *Written by Mangiku*

At Wakanoura:

> Abreast I am at last
> With the fleeting spring
> Here in the open bay
> Of Wakanoura.

I wrote this poem in the temple of Kimiidera overlooking the sea.

Dragging my sore heels, I plodded along like Saigyō, all the time with the memory of his suffering at the River Tenryū in my mind, and when I hired a horse, I thought of the famous priest[27] who had experienced the disgrace of being thrown from his horse into a moat. Nevertheless, it was a great pleasure to see the marvellous beauties of nature, rare scenes in the mountains or along the coast, or to visit the sites of temporary abodes of ancient sages where they had spent secluded lives, or better still, to meet people who had entirely devoted themselves to the search for artistic truth. Since I had nowhere permanent to stay, I had no interest whatever in keeping treasures, and since I was empty-handed, I had no fear of being robbed on the way. I walked at full ease, scorning the pleasure of riding in a palanquin, and filled my hungry stomach with coarse food, shunning the luxury of meat. I bent my steps in whatever direction I wished, having no itinerary to follow. My only mundane concerns were whether I would be able to find a suitable place to sleep at night and whether the straw sandals were the right size for my feet. Every turn of the road brought me new thoughts and every sunrise gave me fresh emotions. My joy was great when I encountered anyone with the slightest understanding of artistic elegance. Even those whom I had long hated for being antiquated and stubborn sometimes proved to be pleasant companions on my wandering journey. Indeed, one of the greatest pleasures of travelling was to find a genius hidden among weeds and bushes, a treasure lost in broken tiles, a mass of gold buried in clay, and when I did find such a person, I always kept a record with the hope that I might be able to show it to my friends.

The day for the spring change of clothing came.

> I took a kimono off
> To feel lighter
> Only putting it in the load
> On my back.

> The moment I descended
> Mount Yoshino,
> I sought to sell
> My cotton-stuffed coat.

Written by Mangiku

I was in Nara on Buddha's birthday, and saw the birth of a fawn. I was so struck by the coincidence that I wrote:

> By what divine consideration
> Is it, I wonder,
> That this fawn is born
> On Buddha's birthday?

Ganjin,[28] founder of the Shōdaiji Temple, is said to have lost his sight on his way to Japan on account of the salt that jumped into his eyes while he endured seventy different trials on the sea. After bowing devoutly before his statue, I wrote:

> If only you allow me,
> I will willingly wipe
> Salt tears from your eyes
> With these fresh leaves.

I parted from an old friend of mine in Nara.

> Just as a stag's antlers
> Are split into tines,
> So I must go willy-nilly
> Separated from my friend.

At a certain man's home in Ōsaka:

> To talk casually
> About an iris flower
> Is one of the pleasures
> Of the wandering journey.

At the beach of Suma:

> The moon is in the sky,
> But as if someone were absent
> The whole scene is empty –
> The summer at Suma.

> I saw the moon,
> But somehow I was left
> Unsatisfied –
> The summer at Suma.

It was in the middle of April when I wandered out to the beach of Suma. The sky was slightly overcast, and the moon on a short night of early summer had special beauty. The mountains were dark with foliage. When I thought it was about time to hear the first voice of the cuckoo, the light of the sun touched the eastern horizon, and as it increased, I began to see on the hills of Ueno ripe ears of wheat tinged with reddish brown and fishermen's huts scattered here and there among the flowers of white poppy.

> At sunrise I saw
> Tanned faces of fishermen
> Among the flowers
> Of white poppy.

There were three villages on this beach, Higashi-suma, Nishi-suma, and Hama-suma. None of these villages, however, seemed to have a distinctive local trade. According to an ancient poet,[29] there used to be a great number of salt farms on the beach, but they must have gone out of existence years before. I saw small fish called *kisugo* spread on the sand to be dried. Some villagers – they hardly seemed professional fishermen – were guarding the fish against the crows that dived to grab them. Each had a bow and arrow in his hand. I wondered why these people still resorted to such a cruel means without the slightest sense of guilt, and thought of the bloody war[30] that had taken place in the mountains at the back of the beach. I wanted to see the site of this old war. So I started to climb Mount Tetsukai. The boy who had been acting as my guide, however, did not like the idea and tried every means to evade it. I coaxed him by saying that I would buy him a dinner after our return, and the boy began to walk, submitting to my request. This boy was sixteen, I was told, but he looked much younger than the other boys I had seen in the village. He walked in front of me, climbing several hundreds of feet through a steep rocky path with many a turn. He slipped countless times, but, always clinging to a root of bamboo or wild azalea, he led the way, completely out of breath and with his brow sweating profusely. It was indeed thanks to this wild effort of the young guide that I was able to reach the gateway of clouds.

> Off the sharp point
> Of a fisherman's arrow
> I heard the cry
> Of a wild cuckoo.

> Where the cuckoo's voice
> Glided into the sea
> Shooting across the sky,
> I found an island.

> In the temple of Suma,
> Under the shade of a tree,
> I thought I had heard
> An ancient flute on the march.

I stopped overnight at Akashi.

> Settled in trap-pots,
> Octopuses may be exulting
> In their ecstasy of a single night
> Under the moon of summer.

It was by a singular stroke of genius that an ancient writer pointed out that autumn was the best season to visit this beach, for it seemed to me that the scene excelled in loneliness and isolation at that season. It was, on the other hand, an incurable folly of mine to think that, had I come here in autumn, I would have had a greater poetic success, for that only proved the poverty of my mind. The island of Awaji lay just across a narrow strip of water and the corresponding hill on the mainland side divided the beach of Suma on the left and that of Akashi on the right. I was reminded of a similar scene on the border of Go and So in China,[31] but a man of greater learning would have thought of many other scenes of a similar nature.

There was a small village called Tai-no-hata in the mountains behind, and this was the birthplace of the two sisters, Matsukaze and Murasame.[32] From this village I followed a narrow ridge road leading to the province of Tamba through many a precipice having such fearful names as Hell's Window[33] and Headlong Fall.[34] When I came to Ichi-no-tani, the huge precipice where Yoshitsune[35] had performed the feat of a downhill rush with great success, I looked down into the valley over the pine tree on which he had hung his war gong and saw the site of his enemy's camp directly below my eyes. The great confusion of the day, together with other tragic incidents of the time, rose afresh in my mind, and I saw before me the aged grandmother of the young emperor taking him in her arms, his mother carrying him on her shoulders, his legs pitifully tangled with her dress, and all of them running into a boat to escape the onslaught of the enemy. Various ladies of the court followed them, and threw into the boat all kinds of things – rare musical instruments, for example – wrapped in sheets and quilts. Many things of value, however, must have fallen overboard – imperial food into the sea for the fish to feed upon, and ladies' vanity boxes on to the sand to be quite forgotten among the grass. This is probably why, even today after a thousand years, the waves break on this beach with such a melancholy sound.

A VISIT TO
SARASHINA VILLAGE

THE autumn wind inspired my heart with a desire to see the rise of the full moon over Mount Obasute. That rugged mountain in the village of Sarashina is where the villagers in the remote past used to abandon their ageing mothers among the rocks. There was another man filled with the same desire, my disciple, Etsujin,[1] who accompanied me, and also a servant sent by my friend Kakei[2] to help me on the journey, for the Kiso road that led to the village was steep and dangerous, passing over a number of high mountains. We all did our best to help one another, but since none of us were experienced travellers, we felt uneasy and made mistakes, doing the wrong things at the wrong times. These mistakes, however, provoked frequent laughter and gave us the courage to push on.

At a certain point on the road, we met an old priest – probably more than sixty years of age – carrying an enormously heavy load on his bent back, tottering along with short, breathless steps and wearing a sullen, serious look on his face. My companions sympathized with him, and, taking the heavy load from the priest's shoulders, put it together with other things they had been carrying on my horse. Consequently, I had to sit on a big pile. Above my head, mountains rose over mountains, and on my left a huge precipice dropped a thousand feet into a boiling river, leaving not a tiny square of flat land in between, so that, perched on the high saddle, I felt stricken with terror every time my horse gave a jerk.

We passed through many a dangerous place, such as Kakehashi, Nezame, Saru-ga-baba, Tachitōge, the road always winding and climbing, so that we often felt as if we were groping our way in the clouds. I abandoned my horse and staggered on my own legs, for I was dizzy with the height and unable to maintain my mental balance from fear. The servant, on the other hand, mounted the horse, and seemed to give not even the slightest thought to the danger. He often nodded in a doze and seemed about to fall headlong over the precipice. Every time I saw him drop his head, I was terrified out of my wits. Upon second thoughts, however, it occurred to me that every one of us was like this servant, wading through the ever-changing reefs of this world in stormy weather, totally blind to the hidden dangers, and that the Buddha surveying us from on high, would surely feel the same misgivings about our fortune as I did about the servant.

When dusk came, we sought a night's lodging in a humble house. After lighting a lamp, I took out my pen and ink, and closed my eyes, trying to remember the sights I had seen and the poems I had composed during the day. When the priest saw me tapping my head and bending over a small piece of paper, he must have thought I was suffering from the weariness of travelling, for he began to give me an account of his youthful pilgrimage, parables from sacred *sutras*, and the stories of the miracles he had witnessed. Alas, I was not able to compose a single poem because of this interruption. Just at this time, however, moonlight touched the corner of my room, coming through the hanging leaves and the chinks in the wall. As I bent my ears to the noise of wooden clappers and the voices of the villagers chasing wild deer away, I felt in my heart that the loneliness of autumn was now consummated in the scene. I said to my companions. 'Let us drink under the bright beams of the moon,' and the master of the house brought out some cups. The cups were too big to be called refined, and were decorated with somewhat uncouth gold-lacquer work, so that over-refined city-dwellers might have hesitated to touch them. Finding them in a remote country as I did, however, I was pleased to see them, and thought that they were even more precious than jewel-inlaid, rare-blue cups.

> Seeing in the country
> A big moon in the sky,
> I felt like decorating it
> With gold-lacquer work.

> On to a bridge
> Suspended over a precipice
> Clings an ivy vine,
> Body and soul together.

> Ancient imperial horses
> Must have also crossed
> This suspended bridge
> On their way to Kyōto.

> Halfway on the bridge,
> I found it impossible
> Even to wink my eye,
> When the fog lifted.   *Written by Etsujin*

Bashō

A poem composed at Mount Obasute:

In imagination,
An old woman and I
Sat together in tears
Admiring the moon.

The moon is already
Sixteen days old,
And yet I linger
In Sarashina Village.

Three days have passed,
And three times I have seen
The bright moon
In the cloudless sky.   *Written by Etsujin*

A yellow valerian
With its slender stalk
Stands bedecked
In droplets of dew.

Hot radish
Pierced my tongue,
While the autumn wind
Pierced my heart.

Horse-chestnuts
From the mountains of Kiso
Will be my presents
To city-dwellers.

A Visit to Sarashina Village

Bidding farewell,
Bidden good-bye,
I walked into
The autumn of Kiso.

A poem composed at Zenkōji Temple:

Four gates
And four different sects
Sleep as one
Under the bright moon.

A sudden storm
Descends on Mount Asama,
Blowing stones
All over me.

THE NARROW ROAD TO THE
DEEP NORTH

Days and months are travellers of eternity. So are the years that pass by. Those who steer a boat across the sea, or drive a horse over the earth till they succumb to the weight of years, spend every minute of their lives travelling. There are a great number of ancients, too, who died on the road. I myself have been tempted for a long time by the cloud-moving wind – filled with a strong desire to wander.

It was only towards the end of last autumn that I returned from rambling along the coast. I barely had time to sweep the cobwebs from my broken house on the River Sumida before the New Year, but no sooner had the spring mist begun to rise over the field than I wanted to be on the road again to cross the barrier-gate of Shirakawa in due time. The gods seemed to have possessed my soul and turned it inside out, and roadside images seemed to invite me from every corner, so that it was impossible for me to stay idle at home. Even while I was getting ready, mending my torn trousers, tying a new strap to my hat, and applying *moxa*[1] to my legs to strengthen them, I was already dreaming of the full moon rising over the islands of Matsushima. Finally, I sold my house, moving to the cottage of Sampū[2] for a temporary stay. Upon the threshold of my old home, however, I wrote a linked verse of eight pieces and hung it on a wooden pillar. The starting piece was:

Behind this door
Now buried in deep grass,
A different generation will celebrate
The Festival of Dolls.[3]

It was early on the morning of March the twenty-seventh that I took to the road. There was darkness lingering in the sky, and the moon was still visible, though gradually thinning away. The faint shadow of Mount Fuji and the cherry blossoms of Ueno and Yanaka were bidding me a last farewell. My friends had got together the night before, and they all came with me on the boat to keep me company for the first few miles. When we got off the boat at Senju, however, the thought of the three thousand miles before me suddenly filled my heart, and neither the houses of the town nor the faces of my friends could be seen by my tearful eyes except as a vision.

The passing spring,
Birds mourn,
Fishes weep
With tearful eyes.

With this poem to commemorate my departure, I walked forth on my journey, but lingering thoughts made my steps heavy. My friends stood in a line and waved good-bye as long as they could see my back.

I walked all through that day, ever wishing to return after seeing the strange sights of the far north, but not really believing in the possibility, for I knew that departing like this on a long journey in the second year of Genroku[4] I should only accumulate more frosty hairs on my head as I approached the colder regions. When I reached the village of Sōka in the evening, my bony shoulders were sore because of the load I had carried, which consisted of a paper coat to keep me warm at night, a light cotton gown to wear after the bath, scanty protection against the rain, writing equipment, and gifts from certain friends of mine. I wanted to travel light, of course, but there were always certain things I could not throw away for either practical or sentimental reasons.

I went to see the shrine of Muro-no-yashima. According to Sora,[5] my companion, this shrine is dedicated to the goddess called the Lady of Flower-bearing Trees,[6] who has another shrine at the foot of Mount Fuji. This goddess is said to have locked herself up in a burning cell to prove the divine nature of her newly-conceived son when her husband doubted it. As a result, her son was named the Lord Born Out of The Fire,[7] and her shrine, Muro-no-yashima, which means a burning cell. It was the custom of this place for poets to sing of the rising smoke, and for ordinary people not to eat *konoshiro*, a speckled fish, which has a vile smell when burnt.

I lodged in an inn at the foot of Mount Nikkō on the

night of March the thirtieth. The host of the inn introduced himself as Honest Gozaemon, and told me to sleep in perfect peace upon his grass pillow, for his sole ambition was to be worthy of his name. I watched him rather carefully but found him almost stubbornly honest, utterly devoid of worldly cleverness. It was as if the merciful Buddha himself had taken the shape of a man to help me in my wandering pilgrimage. Indeed, such saintly honesty and purity as his must not be scorned, for it verges closely on the Perfection preached by Confucius.

On the first day of April, I climbed Mount Nikkō to do homage to the holiest of the shrines upon it. This mountain used to be called Nikō. When the high priest Kūkai[8] built a temple upon it, however, he changed the name to Nikkō, which means the bright beams of the sun. Kūkai must have had the power to see a thousand years into the future, for the mountain is now the seat of the most sacred of all shrines, and its benevolent power prevails throughout the land, embracing the entire people, like the bright beams of the sun. To say more about the shrine would be to violate its holiness.

> It was with awe
> That I beheld
> Fresh leaves, green leaves,
> Bright in the sun.

Mount Kurokami was visible through the mist in the distance. It was brilliantly white with snow in spite of its name, which means black hair.

> Rid of my hair,
> I came to Mount Kurokami,

> On the day we put on
> Clean summer clothes.   *Written by Sora*

My companion's real name is Kawai Sōgorō, Sora being his pen name. He used to live in my neighbourhood and help me in such chores as bringing water and firewood. He wanted to enjoy the views of Matsushima and Kisagata with me, and also to share with me the hardships of the wandering journey. So he took to the road after taking the tonsure on the very morning of our departure, putting on the black robe of an itinerant priest, and even changing his name to Sōgo, which means Religiously Enlightened. His poem, therefore, is not intended as a mere description of Mount Kurokami. The last two lines, in particular, impress us deeply, for they express his determination to persist in his purpose.

After climbing two hundred yards or so from the shrine, I came to a waterfall, which came pouring out of a hollow in the ridge and tumbled down into the dark green pool below in a huge leap of several hundred feet. The rocks of the waterfall were so carved out that we could see it from behind, though hidden ourselves in a craggy cave. Hence its nickname, See-from-behind.[9]

> Silent a while in a cave,
> I watched a waterfall,
> For the first of
> The summer observances.

A friend was living in the town of Kurobane in the province of Nasu. There was a wide expanse of grass-moor, and the town was on the other side of it. I decided to follow a short cut which ran straight for miles and miles across the moor. I noticed a small village in the distance, but before I reached it rain began to fall and darkness closed in. I put up at a solitary farmer's house for the night, and started again early next morning. As I was plodding through the grass, I noticed a horse grazing by the roadside and a farmer cutting grass with a sickle. I asked him to do me the favour of lending me his horse. The farmer hesitated for a while, but finally, with a touch of sympathy in his face, he said to me, 'There are hundreds of crossroads in the grass-moor. A stranger like you can easily go astray. This horse knows the way. You can send him back when he won't go any further.' So I mounted the horse and started off, when

two small children came running after me. One of them was a girl named Kasane, which means manifold. I thought her name was somewhat strange but exceptionally beautiful.

> If your name, Kasane,
> Means manifold,
> How befitting it is also
> For a double-flowered pink. *Written by Sora*

By and by I came to a small village. I therefore sent back the horse, with a small amount of money tied to the saddle.

I arrived safely at the town of Kurobane, and visited my friend, Jōbōji,[10] who was then looking after the mansion of his lord in his absence. He was overjoyed to see me so unexpectedly, and we talked for days and nights together. His brother, Tōsui,[11] seized every opportunity to talk with me, accompanied me to his home and introduced me to his relatives and friends. One day we took a walk to the suburbs. We saw the ruins of an ancient dog-shooting ground,[12] and pushed farther out into the grass-moor to see the tomb of Lady Tamamo[13] and the famous Hachiman Shrine, upon whose god the brave archer, Yoichi,[14] is said to have called for aid when he was challenged to shoot a single fan suspended over a boat drifting offshore. We came home after dark.

I was invited out to Kōmyōji Temple, to visit the hall in which was enshrined the founder of the Shugen sect.[15] He is said to have travelled all over the country in wooden clogs, preaching his doctrines.

> Amid mountains of high summer,
> I bowed respectfully before
> The tall clogs of a statue,
> Asking a blessing on my journey.

There was a Zen temple called Unganji in this province. The Priest Bucchō[16] used to live in isolation in the mountains behind the temple. He once told me that he had written the following poem upon the rock of his hermitage with the charcoal he had made from pine.

This grassy hermitage,
Hardly any more
Than five feet square,
I would gladly quit
But for the rain.

A group of young people accompanied me to the temple. They talked so cheerfully along the way that I reached it before I knew it. The temple was situated on the side of a mountain completely covered with dark cedars and pines. A narrow road trailed up the valley, between banks of dripping moss, leading us to the gate of the temple across a bridge. The air was still cold, though it was April.

I went behind the temple to see the remains of the Priest Bucchō's hermitage. It was a tiny hut propped against the base of a huge rock. I felt as if I were in the presence of the Priest Genmyō's[17] cell or the Priest Hōun's[18] retreat. I hung on a wooden pillar of the cottage the following poem which I wrote impromptu.

Even the woodpeckers
Have left it untouched,
This tiny cottage
In a summer grove.

Taking leave of my friend in Kurobane, I started for the Murder Stone,[19] so called because it killed birds and insects that approached it. I was riding a horse my friend had lent me, when the farmer who led the horse asked me to compose a poem for him. His request came to me as a pleasant surprise.

> Turn the head of your horse
> Sideways across the field,
> To let me hear
> The cry of a cuckoo.

The Murder Stone was in a dark corner of a mountain near a hot spring, and was completely wrapped in the poisonous gas rising from it. There was such a pile of dead bees, butterflies, and other insects, that the real colour of the ground was hardly discernible.

I went to see the willow tree which Saigyō[20] celebrated in his poem, when he wrote, 'Spreading its shade over a crystal stream'. I found it near the village of Ashino on the bank of a rice-field. I had been wondering in my mind where this tree was situated, for the ruler of this province had repeatedly talked to me about it, but this day, for the first time in my life, I had an opportunity to rest my worn-out legs under its shade.

> When the girls had planted
> A square of paddy-field,
> I stepped out of
> The shade of a willow tree.

After many days of solitary wandering, I came at last to the barrier-gate of Shirakawa, which marks the entrance to the northern regions. Here, for the first time, my mind was able to gain a certain balance and composure, no longer a victim to pestering anxiety, so it was with a mild sense of detachment that I thought about the ancient traveller who had passed through this gate with a burning desire to write home. This gate was counted among the three largest checking stations, and many poets had passed through it, each leaving a poem of his own making. I myself walked between trees laden with thick foliage, with the distant sound of autumn wind in my ears and the vision of autumn tints before my eyes. There were hundreds and thousands of pure white blossoms of *unohana*[21] in full bloom on either side of the road, in addition to the equally white blossoms of brambles, so that the ground, at a glance, seemed to be covered with early snow. According to the accounts of Kiyosuke,[22] the ancients are said to have passed through this gate, dressed up in their best clothes.

> Decorating my hair
> With white blossoms of *unohana*,
> I walked through the gate,
> My only gala dress.   *Written by Sora*

Pushing towards the north, I crossed the River Abukuma, and walked between the high mountains of Aizu on the left and the three villages of Iwaki, Sōma, and Miharu on the right, which were divided from the villages of Hitachi and Shimotsuke districts by a range of low mountains. I stopped at the Shadow Pond,[23] so called because it was thought to reflect the exact shadow of any object that approached its shore. It was a cloudy day, however, and nothing but the grey sky was reflected in the pond. I called on the Poet Tōkyū[24] at the post town of Sukagawa, and spent a few days at his house. He asked me how I had fared at the gate of Shirakawa. I had to tell him that I had not been able to make as many poems as I wanted, partly because I had been absorbed in the wonders of the surrounding countryside and the recollections of ancient poets. It was deplorable, however, to have passed the gate of Shirakawa without a single poem worth recording, so I wrote:

> The first poetic venture
> I came across –
> The rice-planting songs
> Of the far north.

Using this poem as a starting piece, we made three books of linked verse.

There was a huge chestnut tree on the outskirts of this post town, and a priest was living in seclusion under its shade.

When I stood there in front of the tree, I felt as if I were in the midst of the deep mountains where the Poet Saigyō had picked nuts. I took a piece of paper from my bag, and wrote as follows:

The chestnut is a holy tree, for the Chinese ideograph for chestnut is Tree placed directly below West, the direction of the holy land. The Priest Gyōki[25] is said to have used it for his walking stick and the chief support of his house.

> The chestnut by the eaves
> In magnificent bloom
> Passes unnoticed
> By men of this world.

Passing through the town of Hiwada, which was about five miles from the house of the Poet Tōkyū, I came to the famous hills of Asaka. The hills were not very far from the highroad, and scattered with numerous pools. It was the season of a certain species of iris called *katsumi*. So I went to look for it. I went from pool to pool, asking every soul I met on the way where I could possibly find it, but strangely enough, no one had ever heard of it, and the sun went down before I caught even a glimpse of it. I cut across to the right at Nihonmatsu, saw the ancient cave of *kurozuka* in a hurry, and put up for the night in Fukushima.

On the following morning I made my way to the village of Shinobu to look at the stone upon whose chequered face they used to dye a certain type of cloth called *shinobu-zuri*. I found the stone in the middle of a small village, half buried in the ground. According to the child who acted as a self-appointed guide, this stone was once on the top of a mountain, but the travellers who came to see it did so much harm to the crops that the farmers thought it a nuisance and thrust it down into the valley, where it rests now with its chequered face downward. I thought the story was not altogether unbelievable.

> The busy hands
> Of rice-planting girls,
> Reminiscent somehow
> Of the old dyeing technique.

Crossing the ferry of Moon Halo,[26] I came to the post town of Rapids Head.[27] The ruined house of the brave warrior Satō[28] was about a mile and a half from this post town towards the foot of the mountains on the left. I pushed my way towards the village of Iizuka, and found a hill called Maruyama in the open field of Sabano. This was the site of the warrior's house. I could not refrain from weeping, when I saw the remains of the front gate at the foot of the hill. There was a lonely temple in the vicinity, and tombs of the Satō family were still standing in the graveyard. I wept bitterly in front of the tombstones of the two young wives, remembering how they had dressed up their frail bodies in armour after the death of their husbands. In fact I felt as if I were in the presence of the Weeping Tombstone of China.[29]

I went into the temple to have a drink of tea. Among the treasures of the temple were the sword of Lord Yoshitsune[30] and the satchel which his faithful retainer, Benkei,[31] had carried on his back.

> Proudly exhibit
> With flying banners
> The sword and the satchel
> This May Festival Day.[32]

I wrote this poem because it was the first day of May. I stopped overnight at Iizuka.

I had a bath in a hot spring before I took shelter at an inn. It was a filthy place with rough straw mats spread out on an earth floor. They had to prepare my bed by the dim light of the fire, for there was not even a lamp in the whole house. A storm came upon us towards midnight, and between the noise of thunder and leaking rain and the raids of mosquitoes and fleas, I could not get a wink of sleep. Furthermore, an attack of my old complaint made me so ill that I left the inn upon the first hint of light in the morning. I suffered severely from repeated attacks while I rode on horseback bound for the town of Kōri. It was indeed a terrible thing to be so ill on the road, when there still remained thousands of miles before me, but thinking that if I were to die on my way to the extreme north it would only be the fulfilment of providence, I trod the earth as firmly as possible and arrived at the barrier-gate of Ōkido in the province of Date.

Passing through the castle towns of Abumizuri and Shiroishi, I arrived at the province of Kasajima, where I asked the way to the mound of Lord Sanekata of the Fujiwara family.[33] I was told that I must turn right in the direction of the villages of Minowa and Kasajima visible at the foot of the mountains in the distance, and that the mound was still there by the side of a shrine, buried in deep grass. I wanted to go that way, of course, but the muddy road after the early rain of the wet season and my own weakness stopped me. The names of the two villages were so befitting to the wet season with their echoes of raincoat and umbrella that I wrote:

> How far must I walk
> To the village of Kasajima
> This endlessly muddy road
> Of the early wet season?

I stopped overnight at Iwanuma.

My heart leaped with joy when I saw the celebrated pine tree of Takekuma, its twin trunks shaped exactly as described by the ancient poets. I was immediately reminded of the Priest Nōin[34] who had grieved to find upon his second visit this same tree cut and thrown into the River Natori as bridge-piles by the newly-appointed governor of the province. This tree had been planted, cut, and replanted several times in the past, but just when I came to see it myself, it was in its original shape after a lapse of perhaps a thousand years, the most beautiful shape one could possibly think of for a pine tree. The Poet Kyohaku[35] wrote as follows at the time of my departure to express his good wishes for my journey.

> Don't forget to show my master
> The famous pine of Takekuma,
> Late cherry blossoms
> Of the far north.

The following poem I wrote was, therefore, a reply.

> Three months after we saw
> Cherry blossoms together
> I came to see the glorious
> Twin trunks of the pine.

Crossing the River Natori, I entered the city of Sendai on May the fourth, the day we customarily throw fresh leaves of iris on the roof and pray for good health. I found an inn, and decided to stay there for several days. There was in this city a painter named Kaemon.[36] I made special efforts to meet him, for he was reputed to be a man with a truly artistic mind. One day he took me to various places of interest which I might have missed but for his assistance. We first went to the plain of Miyagino, where fields of bush-clover were waiting to blossom in autumn. The hills of Tamada, Yokono, and Tsutsuji-ga-oka were covered with white rhododendrons in bloom. Then we went into the dark pine woods called Konoshita where even the beams of the sun could not penetrate. This darkest spot on the earth had often been a subject of poetry because of its dewiness – for example, one poet says that his lord needs an umbrella to protect him from the drops of dew when he enters it. We also stopped at the shrines of Yakushidō and Tenjin on our way home. When the time came for us to say good-bye, this painter gave me his own drawings of Matsu-shima and Shiogama and two pairs of straw sandals with laces dyed in the deep blue of the iris. In this last appears most clearly perhaps the true artistic nature of this man.

> It looks as if
> Iris flowers had bloomed
> On my feet –
> Sandals laced in blue.

Relying solely on the drawings of Kaemon which served as a guide, I pushed along the Narrow Road to the Deep North, and came to the place where tall sedges were grow-ing in clusters. This was the home of the famous sedge-mats of Tofu. Even now it is the custom of the people of this area to send carefully woven mats as a tribute to the governor each year.

I found the stone monument of Tsubo-no-ishibumi on the ancient site of the Taga castle in the village of Ichikawa. The monument was about six feet tall and three feet wide, and the engraved letters were still visible on its surface through thick layers of moss. In addition to the numbers giving the mileage to various provinces, it was possible to read the following words.

This castle was built upon the present site in the first year of Jinki[37] by General Ōno-no-Azumabito[38] dispatched to the Northern Provinces by His Majesty, and remodelled in the sixth year of Tempyōhōji[39] by His Majesty's Councillor and General Emi-no-Asakari,[40] Governor of the Eastern and Northern Provinces.

According to the date given at the end of the inscription, this monument was erected during the reign of Emperor Shōmu,[41] and had stood here ever since, winning the ever-increasing admiration of poets through the years. In this ever-changing world where mountains crumble, rivers change their courses, roads are deserted, rocks are buried, and old trees yield to young shoots, it was nothing short of a miracle that this monument alone had survived the battering of a thousand years to be the living memory of the ancients. I felt as if I were in the presence of the ancients themselves, and, forgetting all the troubles I had suffered on the road, rejoiced in the utter happiness of this joyful moment, not without tears in my eyes.

Stopping briefly at the River Noda-no-tamagawa and the so-called Rock in the Offing,[42] I came to the pine woods called Sue-no-matsuyama, where I found a temple named

Masshōzan and a great number of tombstones scattered among the trees. It was a depressing sight indeed, for young or old, loved or loving, we must all go to such a place at the end of our lives. I entered the town of Shiogama, hearing the ding-dong of the curfew. Above was the darkening sky unusually empty for May, and beyond was the silhouette of Magaki-ga-shima Island not far from the shore in the moonlight. The voices of the fishermen dividing the catch of the day made me even more lonely, for I was immediately reminded of an old poem which pitied them for their precarious lives on the sea. Later in the evening, I had a chance to hear a blind minstrel singing to his lute. His songs were different from either the narrative songs of the Heike[43] or the traditional songs of dancing, and were called *Okujōruri* (*Dramatic Narratives of the Far North*). I must confess that the songs were a bit too boisterous, when chanted so near my ears, but I found them not altogether unpleasing, for they still retained the rustic flavours of the past.

The following morning, I rose early and did homage to the great god of the Myōjin Shrine of Shiogama. This shrine had been rebuilt by a former governor of the province with stately columns, painted beams and an impressive stone approach, and the morning sun shining directly on the vermilion fencing was almost dazzlingly bright. I was deeply impressed by the fact that the divine power of the gods had penetrated even to the extreme north of our country, and I bowed in humble reverence before the altar. I noticed an old lantern in front of the shrine. According to the inscription on its iron window, it was dedicated by Izumi-no-Saburō[44] in the third year of Bunji.[45] My thought immediately flew back across the span of five hundred years to the days of this most faithful warrior. His life is certain evidence that, if one performs one's duty and maintains one's loyalty, fame comes naturally in the wake, for there is hardly anyone now who does not honour him as the flower of chivalry.

It was already close to noon when I left the shrine. I hired a boat and started for the islands of Matsushima. After two miles or so on the sea, I landed on the sandy beach of Ojima Island.

Much praise had already been lavished upon the wonders of the islands of Matsushima. Yet if further praise is possible, I would like to say that here is the most beautiful spot in the whole country of Japan, and that the beauty of these islands is not in the least inferior to the beauty of Lake Dōtei[46] or Lake Seiko[47] in China. The islands are situated in a bay about three miles wide in every direction and open to the sea through a narrow mouth on the south-east side. Just as the River Sekkō[48] in China is made full at each swell of the tide, so is this bay filled with the brimming water of the ocean, and innumerable islands are scattered over it from one end to the other. Tall islands point to the sky and level ones prostrate themselves before the surges of water. Islands are piled above islands, and islands are joined to islands, so that they look exactly like parents caressing their children or walking with them arm in arm. The pines are of the freshest green, and their branches are curved in exquisite lines, bent by the wind constantly blowing through them. Indeed, the beauty of the entire scene can only be compared to the most divinely endowed of feminine countenances, for who else could have created such beauty but the great god of nature himself? My pen strove in vain to equal this superb creation of divine artifice.

Ojima Island where I landed was in reality a peninsula projecting far out into the sea. This was the place where the Priest Ungo[49] had once retired, and the rock on which he used to sit for meditation was still there. I noticed a number of tiny cottages scattered among pine trees and pale blue threads of smoke rising from them. I wondered what kind of people were living in those isolated houses, and was approaching one of them with a strange sense of yearning, when, as if to interrupt me, the moon rose glittering over the darkened sea, completing the full transformation to a night-time scene. I lodged in an inn overlooking the bay, and went to bed in my upstairs room with all the windows open. As I lay there in the midst of the roaring wind and driving clouds, I felt myself to be in a world totally different from the one I was accustomed to. My companion Sora wrote:

> Clear voiced cuckoo,
> Even you will need
> The silver wings of a crane
> To span the islands of Matsushima.

I myself tried to fall asleep, supressing the surge of emotion from within, but my excitement was simply too great. I finally took out my notebook from my bag and read the poems given me by my friends at the time of my departure – a Chinese poem by Sodō,[50] a *waka* by Hara Anteki,[51] *haiku* by Sampū and Dakushi,[52] all about the islands of Matsushima.

I went to Zuiganji Temple on the eleventh. This temple was founded by Makabe-no-Heishirō[53] after he had become a priest and returned from China, and was later enlarged by the Priest Ungo into a massive temple with seven stately halls embellished with gold. The priest I met at the temple was the thirty-second in descent from the founder. I also wondered in my mind where the temple of the much-admired Priest Kenbutsu[54] could have been situated.

I left for Hiraizumi on the twelfth. I wanted to see the pine tree of Aneha and the bridge of Odae on my way. So I followed a lonely mountain trail trodden only by hunters and woodcutters, but somehow I lost my way and came to the port of Ishinomaki. The port was located in a spacious bay, across which lay the island of Kinkazan, an old gold-mine once celebrated as 'blooming with flowers of gold'.[55] There were hundreds of ships, large and small, anchored in the harbour, and countless streaks of smoke continually rising from the houses that thronged the shore. I was pleased to see this busy place, though it was mere chance that had brought me here, and began to look for a suitable place to stay. Strangely enough, however, no one offered me hospitality. After much inquiring, I found a miserable house, and, spending an uneasy night, I wandered out again on the following morning on a road that was totally un-known to me. Looking across to the ford of Sode, the meadow of Obuchi and the pampas-moor of Mano, I pushed along the road that formed the embankment of a river. Sleeping overnight at Toima, where the long swampish river came to an end at last, I arrived at Hiraizumi after wandering some twenty miles in two days.

It is here that the glory of the three generations of the Fujiwara family[56] passed away like a snatch of empty dream. The ruins of the main gate greeted my eyes a mile before I came upon Lord Hidehira's mansion, which had been utterly reduced to rice-paddies. Mount Kinkei alone retained its original shape. As I climbed one of the foothills called Takadate, where Lord Yoshitsune met his death, I saw the River Kitakami running through the plains of Nambu in its full force, and its tributary, Koromogawa, winding along the site of the Izumi-ga-shiro castle and pouring into the big river directly below my eyes. The ruined house of Lord Yasuhira was located to the north of the barrier-gate of Koromo-ga-seki, thus blocking the entrance from the Nambu area and forming a protection against barbarous intruders from the north. Indeed, many a feat of chivalrous valour was repeated here during the short span of the three generations, but both the actors and the deeds have long been dead and passed into oblivion. When a country is defeated, there remain only mountains and rivers, and on a ruined castle in spring only grasses thrive. I sat down on my hat and wept bitterly till I almost forgot time.

> A thicket of summer grass
> Is all that remains
> Of the dreams and ambitions
> Of ancient warriors.

I caught a glimpse
Of the frosty hair of Kanefusa[57]
Wavering among
The white blossoms of *unohana*.

Written by Sora

The interiors of the two sacred buildings of whose wonders I had often heard with astonishment were at last revealed to me. In the library of *sutras* were placed the statues of the three nobles who governed this area, and enshrined in the so-called Gold Chapel[58] were the coffins containing their bodies, and three sacred images. These buildings, too, would have perished under the all-devouring grass, their treasures scattered, their jewelled doors broken and their gold pillars crushed, but thanks to the outer frame and a covering of tiles added for protection, they had survived to be a monument of at least a thousand years.

Even the long rain of May
Has left it untouched –
This Gold Chapel
Aglow in the sombre shade.

Turning away from the highroad leading to the provinces of Nambu, I came to the village of Iwate, where I stopped overnight. The next day, I looked at the cape of Oguro and the tiny island of Mizu, both in a river, and arrived by way of Naruko hot spring at the barrier-gate of Shitomae which blocked the entrance to the province of Dewa. The gate-keepers were extremely suspicious, for very few travellers dared to pass this difficult road under normal circumstances. I was admitted after long waiting,

so that darkness overtook me while I was climbing a huge mountain. I put up at a gate-keeper's house which I was very lucky to find in such a lonely place. A storm came upon us and I was held up for three days.

> Bitten by fleas and lice,
> I slept in a bed,
> A horse urinating all the time
> Close to my pillow.

According to the gate-keeper, there was a huge body of mountains obstructing my way to the province of Dewa, and the road was terribly uncertain. So I decided to hire a guide. The gate-keeper was kind enough to find me a young man of tremendous physique, who walked in front of me with a curved sword strapped at his waist and a stick of oak gripped firmly in his hand. I myself followed him, afraid of what might happen on the way. What the gate-keeper had told me turned out to be true. The mountains were so thickly covered with foliage and the air underneath was so hushed that I felt as if I were groping my way in the dead of night. There was not even the cry of a single bird

to be heard, and the wind seemed to breathe out black soot through every rift in the hanging clouds. I pushed my way through thick undergrowth of bamboo, crossing many streams and stumbling over hidden rocks, till at last I arrived at the village of Mogami after much shedding of cold sweat. My guide congratulated me by saying that I was indeed fortunate to have crossed the mountains in safety, for accidents of some sort had always happened on his past trips. I thanked him sincerely and parted from him. However, fear lingered in my mind some time after that.

I visited Seifū[59] in the town of Obanazawa. He was a rich merchant and yet a man of a truly poetic turn of mind. He had a deep understanding of the hardships of the wandering journey, for he himself travelled frequently to the capital city. He invited me to stay at his place as long as I wished and tried to make me comfortable in every way he could.

> I felt quite at home,
> As if it were mine,
> Sleeping lazily
> In this house of fresh air.

Crawl out bravely
And show me your face,
The solitary voice of a toad
Beneath the silkworm nursery.

With a powder-brush
Before my eyes,
I strolled among
Rouge-plants.

In the silkworm nursery,
Men and women
Are dressed
Like gods in ancient times.   *Written by Sora*

There was a temple called Ryūshakuji in the province of Yamagata. Founded by the great Priest Jikaku,[60] this temple was known for the absolute tranquillity of its holy compound. Since everybody advised me to see it, I changed my course at Obanazawa and went there, though it meant walking an extra seven miles or so. When I reached it, the late afternoon sun was still lingering over the scene. After arranging to stay with the priests at the foot of the mountain, I climbed to the temple situated near the summit. The whole mountain was made of massive rocks thrown together, and covered with age-old pines and oaks. The stony ground itself bore the colour of eternity, paved with velvety moss. The doors of the shrines built on the rocks were firmly barred and there was not a sound to be heard. As I moved on all fours from rock to rock, bowing reverently at each shrine, I felt the purifying power of this holy environment pervading my whole being.

> In the utter silence
> Of a temple,
> A cicada's voice alone
> Penetrates the rocks.

I wanted to sail down the River Mogami, but while I was waiting for fair weather at Ōishida, I was told that the old seed of linked verse once strewn here by the scattering wind had taken root, still bearing its own flowers each year and thus softening the minds of the rough villagers like the clear note of a reedpipe, but that these rural poets were now merely struggling to find their way in the forest of error, unable to distinguish between the new and the old style, for there was no one to guide them. At their request, therefore, I sat with them to compose a book of linked verse, and left it behind me as a gift. It was indeed a great pleasure for me to be of such help during my wandering journey.

The River Mogami rises in the high mountains of the far north, and its upper course runs through the province of Yamagata. There are many dangerous spots along this river, such as Speckled Stones[61] and Eagle Rapids,[62] but it finally empties itself into the sea at Sakata, after washing the north edge of Mount Itajiki. As I descended this river in a boat, I felt as if the mountains on both sides were ready to fall down upon me, for the boat was a tiny one – the kind that the farmers had used for carrying sheaves of rice in old times – and the trees were heavily laden with foliage. I saw the Cascade of Silver Threads[63] sparkling through the green leaves and the temple called Sennindō standing close to the shore. The river was swollen to the brim, and the boat was in constant peril.

Gathering all the rains
Of May,
The River Mogami rushes down
In one violent stream.

I climbed Mount Haguro on the third of June. Through the effort of my friend, Zushi Sakichi,[64] I was granted an audience with the high priest Egaku,[65] then presiding over this whole mountain temple as acting bishop. He received me kindly and gave me a comfortable lodging in one of the annexes in the South Valley.

On the following day, I sat with the priest in the main hall to compose some linked verse. I wrote:

Blessed indeed
Is this South Valley,
Where the gentle wind breathes
The faint aroma of snow.

I visited the Gongen Shrine on the fifth. The founder of this shrine is the priest called Nōjo,[66] but no one knows exactly when he lived. *Court Ceremonies and Rites during the Years of Engi,*[67] however, mentions that there is a sacred shrine on Mount Sato in the province of Dewa. The scribe must have written Sato where he should have written Kuro, for the two sounds are represented by Chinese ideographs looking very much alike. The present name of the mountain, Haguro, is probably an abridged form of Mount Kuro in the province Dewa. According to a local history book, the name of the province itself is derived from the fact that quantities of feathers were sent to the Emperor each year as a tribute from this province. Be that as it may, this shrine on Mount Haguro is counted among the three most sacred shrines of the north, together with the shrines on Mount Gassan and Mount Yudono, and is a sister shrine of the temple on Mount Tōei in Edo. Here the Doctrine of Absolute Meditation preached in the Tendai sect[68] shines forth like the clear beams of the moon, and the Laws of Spiritual Freedom and Enlightenment illuminate as lamps in utter darkness. There are hundreds of houses where the priests practise religious rites with absolute severity. Indeed the whole mountain is filled with miraculous inspiration and sacred awe. Its glory will never perish as long as man continues to live on the earth.

I climbed Mount Gassan on the eighth. I tied around my neck a sacred rope made of white paper and covered my head with a hood made of bleached cotton, and set off with my guide on a long march of eight miles to the top of the mountain. I walked through mists and clouds, breathing the thin air of high altitudes and stepping on slippery ice and snow, till at last through a gateway of clouds, as it seemed, to the very paths of the sun and moon, I reached the summit, completely out of breath and nearly frozen to death. Presently the sun went down and the moon rose glistening in the sky. I spread some leaves on the ground and went to sleep, resting my head on pliant bamboo branches. When, on the following morning, the sun rose again and dispersed the clouds, I went down towards Mount Yudono.

As I was still descending, I saw an old smithy built right on a trickling stream. According to my guide, this is where Gassan,[69] a local swordsmith, used to make his swords, tempering them in the crystal-clear water of the stream.

He made his swords with such skill and devotion that they became famous throughout the world. He must have chosen this particular spot for his smithy probably because he knew of a certain mysterious power latent in the water, just as indeed a similar power is known to have existed in the water of Ryōsen Spring[70] in China. Nor is the story of Kanshō and Bakuya[71] out of place here, for it also teaches us that no matter where your interest lies, you will not be able to accomplish anything unless you bring your deepest devotion to it. As I sat reflecting thus upon a rock, I saw in front of me a cherry tree hardly three feet tall just beginning to blossom – far behind the season of course, but victorious against the heavy weight of snow which it had resisted for more than half a year. I immediately thought of the famous Chinese poem about 'the plum tree fragrant in the blazing heat of summer'[72] and of an equally pathetic poem by the Priest Gyōson, [73] and felt even more attached to the cherry tree in front of me. I saw many other things of interest in this mountain, the details of which, however, I refrain from betraying in accordance with the rules I must obey as a pilgrim. When I returned to my lodging, my host, Egaku, asked me to put down in verse some impressions of my pilgrimage to the three mountains, so I wrote as follows on the narrow strips of writing paper he had given me.

> How cool it is,
> A pale crescent shining
> Above the dark hollow
> Of Mount Haguro.

> How many columns of clouds
> Had risen and crumbled, I wonder

Before the silent moon rose
Over Mount Gassan.

Forbidden to betray
The holy secrets of Mount Yudono,
I drenched my sleeves
In a flood of reticent tears.

Tears rushed to my eyes
As I stepped knowingly
Upon the coins on the sacred road
Of Mount Yudono.   *Written by Sora*

Leaving Mount Haguro on the following day, I came to
the castle town called Tsuru-ga-oka, where I was received
warmly by Nagayama Shigeyuki,[74] a warrior, and com-
posed a book of linked verse with him and Zushi Sakichi
who had accompanied me all the way from Mount
Haguro. Bidding them farewell, I again descended the

River Mogami in a boat and arrived at the port of Sakata,
where I was entertained by the physician named En'an
Fugyoku.[75]

I enjoyed the evening cool
Along the windy beach of Fukuura,

Behind me, Mount Atsumi
Still in the hot sun.

The River Mogami has drowned
Far and deep
Beneath its surging waves
The flaming sun of summer.

    I had seen since my departure innumerable examples of natural beauty which land and water, mountains and rivers, had produced in one accord, and yet in no way could I suppress the great urge I had in my mind to see the miraculous beauty of Kisagata, a lagoon situated to the north-east of Sakata. I followed a narrow trail for about ten miles, climbing steep hills, descending to rocky shores, or pushing through sandy beaches, but just about the time the dim sun was nearing the horizon, a strong wind rose from the sea, blowing up fine grains of sand, and rain, too, began to spread a grey film of cloud across the sky, so that even Mount Chōkai was made invisible. I walked in this state of semi-blindness, picturing all sorts of views to myself, till at last I put up at a fisherman's hut, convinced that if there was so much beauty in the dark rain, much more was promised by fair weather.

    A clear sky and brilliant sun greeted my eyes on the following morning, and I sailed across the lagoon in an open boat. I first stopped at a tiny island named after the Priest Nōin[76] to have a look at his retreat where he had stayed for three years, and then landed on the opposite shore where there was the aged cherry tree which Saigyō[77] honoured by writing 'sailing over the waves of blossoms'. There were also a mausoleum of the Empress Jingū[78] and the temple named Kanmanjuji. I was a bit surprised to hear of her visit here and left in doubt as to its historical truth, but I sat in a spacious room of the temple to command the entire view of the lagoon. When the hanging screens were rolled up, an extraordinary view unfolded itself before my eyes – Mount Chōkai supporting the sky like a pillar in the south with its shadowy reflection in the water, the barrier-gate of Muyamuya just visible in the west, an endless causeway leading as far as Akita in the east, and finally in the north, Shiogoshi, the mouth of the lagoon with waves of the outer ocean breaking against it. Although little more than a mile in width, this lagoon is not in the least inferior to Matsushima in charm and grace. There is, however, a remarkable difference between the two. Matsushima is a cheerful laughing beauty, while the charm of Kisagata is in the beauty of its weeping countenance. It is not only lonely but also penitent, as it were, for some unknown evil. Indeed it has a striking resemblance to the expression of a troubled mind.

> A flowering silk tree
> In the sleepy rain of Kisagata
> Reminds me of Lady Seishi
> In sorrowful lament.[79]

> Cranes hop around
> On the watery beach of Shiogoshi
> Dabbling their long legs
> In the cool tide of the sea.

> What special delicacy
> Is served here, I wonder,

Coming to Kisagata
On a festival day.   *Written by Sora*

Sitting at full ease
On the doors of their huts,
The fishermen enjoy
A cool evening.   *Written by Teiji,*[80] *a merchant
from the province of Mino*

A poem for a pair of faithful osprey nesting on a rock:

What divine instinct
Has taught these birds
No waves swell so high
As to swamp their home?   *Written by Sora*

After lingering in Sakata for several days, I left on a long
walk of one hundred and thirty miles to the capital of the
province of Kaga. As I looked up at the clouds gathering
around the mountains of the Hokuriku road, the thought
of the great distance awaiting me almost overwhelmed my
heart. Driving myself all the time, however, I entered the
province of Echigo through the barrier-gate of Nezu, and
arrived at the barrier-gate of Ichiburi in the province of
Ecchū. During the nine days I needed for this trip, I could
not write very much, what with the heat and moisture, and
my old complaint that pestered me immeasurably.

The night looks different
Already on July the sixth,
For tomorrow, once a year
The Weaver meets her lover.[81]

The great Milky Way
Spans in a single arch
The billow-crested sea,
Falling on Sado beyond.

Exhausted by the labour of crossing many dangerous places by the sea with such horrible names as Children-desert-parents[82] or Parents-desert-children,[83] Dog-denying[84] or Horse-repelling,[85] I went to bed early when I reached the barrier-gate of Ichiburi. The voices of two young women whispering in the next room, however, came creeping into my ears. They were talking to an elderly man, and I gathered from their whispers that they were concubines from Niigata in the province of Echigo, and that the old man, having accompanied them here on their way to the Ise Shrine, was going home the next day with their messages to their relatives and friends. I sympathized with them, for as they said themselves among their whispers, their life was such that they had to drift along even as the white froth of waters that beat on the shore, and having been forced to find a new companion each night, they had to renew their pledge of love at every turn, thus proving each time the fatal sinfulness of their nature. I listened to their whispers till fatigue lulled me to sleep.

When, on the following morning, I stepped into the road, I met these women again. They approached me and said with some tears in their eyes, 'We are forlorn travellers, complete strangers on this road. Will you be kind enough at least to let us follow you? If you are a priest as your black robe tells us, have mercy on us and help us to learn the great love of our Saviour.' 'I am greatly touched by your words,' I said in reply after a moment's thought, 'but we have so many places to stop at on the way that we cannot help you. Go as other travellers go. If you have trust in the Saviour, you will never lack His divine protection.' As I stepped away from them, however, my heart was filled with persisting pity.

> Under the same roof
> We all slept together,
> Concubines and I –
> Bush-clovers and the moon.

As I recited this poem to Sora, he immediately put it down on his notebook.

Crossing the so-called forty-eight rapids of the Kurobe River and countless other streams, I came to the village of Nago, where I inquired after the famous wisteria vines of Tako, for I wanted to see them in their early autumn colours though their flowering season was spring. The villager answered me, however, that they were beyond the mountain in the distance about five miles away along the coastline, completely isolated from human abode, so that not a single fisherman's hut was likely to be found to give me a night's lodging. Terrified by these words, I walked straight into the province of Kaga.

I walked into the fumes
Of early-ripening rice,
On the right below me
The waters of the Angry Sea.[86]

Across the mountains of Unohana-yama and the valleys
of Kurikara-dani, I entered the city of Kanazawa on July
the fifteenth, where I met a merchant from Ōsaka named
Kashō[87] who invited me to stay at his inn.

There was in this city a man named Isshō[88] whose
unusual love of poetry had gained him a lasting reputation
among the verse-writers of the day. I was told, however,
that he had died unexpectedly in the winter of the past
year. I attended the memorial service held for him by his
brother.

Move, if you can hear,
Silent mound of my friend,
My wails and the answering
Roar of autumn wind.

A visit to a certain hermitage:

On a cool autumn day,
Let us peel with our hands
Cucumbers and mad-apples
For our simple dinner.

A poem composed on the road:

Red, red is the sun,
Heartlessly indifferent to time,
The wind knows, however,
The promise of early chill.

At the place called Dwarfed Pine:[89]

> Dwarfed Pine is indeed
> A gentle name, and gently
> The wind brushes through
> Bush-clovers and pampas.

I went to the Tada Shrine situated in the vicinity, where I saw Lord Sanemori's[90] helmet and a piece of brocaded cloth that he had worn under his armour. According to the legend, these were given him by Lord Yoshitomo[91] while he was still in the service of the Minamotos.[92] The helmet was certainly an extraordinary one, with an arabesque of gold chrysanthemums covering the visor and the ear-plate, a fiery dragon resting proudly on the crest, and two curved horns pointing to the sky. The chronicle of the shrine gave a vivid account of how, upon the heroic death of Lord Sanemori, Kiso Yoshinaka[93] had sent his important retainer Higuchi-no-Jirō[94] to the shrine to dedicate the helmet with a letter of prayer.

> I am awe-struck
> To hear a cricket singing
> Underneath the dark cavity
> Of an old helmet.

On my way to the Yamanaka hot spring, the white peak of Mount Shirane overlooked me all the time from behind. At last I came to the spot where there was a temple hard by a mountain on the left. According to the legend this temple was built to enshrine Kannon, the great goddess of mercy, by the Emperor Kazan,[95] when he had finished his round of the so-called Thirty-three Sacred Temples, and its name

Nata was compounded of Nachi and Tanigumi, the first and last of these temples respectively. There were beautiful rocks and old pines in the garden, and the goddess was placed in the thatched house built on a rock. Indeed, the entire place was filled with strange sights.

> Whiter far
> Than the white rocks
> Of the Rock Temple
> The autumn wind blows.

I enjoyed a bath in the hot spring whose marvellous properties had a reputation of being second to none, except the hot spring of Ariake.[96]

> Bathed in such comfort
> In the balmy spring of Yamanaka,
> I can do without plucking
> Life-preserving chrysanthemums.

The host of the inn was a young man named Kumenosuke.[97] His father was a poet, and there was an interesting story about him: one day, when Teishitsu[98] (later a famous poet in Kyōto but a young man then) came to this place, he met this man and suffered a terrible humiliation because of his ignorance of poetry, and so upon his return to Kyōto, he became a student of Teitoku[99] and never abandoned his studies in poetry till he had established himself as an independent poet. It was generally believed that Teishitsu gave instruction in poetry free of charge to anyone from this village throughout his life. It must be admitted, however, that this is already a story of long ago.

My companion, Sora, was seized with an incurable pain

in his stomach. So he decided to hurry, all by himself, to his relatives in the village of Nagashima in the province of Ise. As he said good-bye, he wrote:

> No matter where I fall
> On the road,
> Fall will I to be buried
> Among flowering bush-clovers.

I felt deeply in my heart both the sorrow of one that goes and the grief of one that remains, just as a solitary bird separated from his flock in dark clouds, and wrote in answer:

> From this day forth, alas,
> The dew-drops shall wash away
> The letters on my hat
> Saying 'A party of two'.

I stopped overnight at the Zenshōji Temple near the castle of Daishōji, still in the province of Kaga. Sora, too, had stayed here the night before and left behind the following poem:

> All night long
> I listened to the autumn wind
> Howling on the hill
> At the back of the temple.

Sora and I were separated by the distance of a single night, but it was just the same as being separated by a thousand miles. I, too, went to bed amidst the howling of the autumn wind and woke up early the next morning amid the chanting of the priests, which was soon followed by the noise of the gong calling us to breakfast. As I was anxious to cross over to the province of Echizen in the course of the day, I left the temple without lingering, but when I reached the foot of the long approach to the temple, a young priest came running down the steps with a brush and ink and asked me to leave a poem behind. As I happened to notice some leaves of willow scattered in the garden, I wrote impromptu,

> I hope to have gathered
> To repay your kindness
> The willow leaves
> Scattered in the garden.

and left the temple without even taking time to refasten my straw sandals.

Hiring a boat at the port of Yoshizaki on the border of the province of Echizen, I went to see the famous pine of

Shiogoshi. The entire beauty of this place, I thought, was best expressed in the following poem by Saigyō.

> Inviting the wind to carry
> Salt waves of the sea,
> The pine tree of Shiogoshi
> Trickles all night long
> Shiny drops of moonlight.

Should anyone dare to write another poem on this pine tree, it would be like trying to add a sixth finger to his hand.

I went to the Tenryūji Temple in the town of Matsuoka, for the head priest of the temple was an old friend of mine. A poet named Hokushi[100] had accompanied me here from Kanazawa, though he had never dreamed of coming this far when he had taken to the road. Now at last he made up his mind to go home, having composed a number of beautiful poems on the views we had enjoyed together. As I said good-bye to him, I wrote:

> Farewell, my old fan.
> Having scribbled on it,
> What could I do but tear it
> At the end of summer?

Making a detour of about a mile and a half from the town of Matsuoka, I went to the Eiheiji Temple. I thought it was nothing short of a miracle that the Priest Dōgen[101] had chosen such a secluded place for the site of the temple.

The distance to the city of Fukui was only three miles. Leaving the temple after supper, however, I had to walk along the darkening road with uncertain steps. There was in this city a poet named Tōsai[102] whom I had seen in Edo some ten years before. Not knowing whether he was already dead or still keeping his bare skin and bones, I went to see him, directed by a man whom I happened to meet on the road. When I came upon a humble cottage in a back street, separated from other houses by a screen of moon-flowers and creeping gourds and a thicket of cockscomb and goosefoot left to grow in front, I knew it was my friend's house. As I knocked at the door, a sad-looking woman peeped out and asked me whether I was a priest and where I had come from. She then told me that the master of the house had gone to a certain place in town, and that I had better see him there if I wanted to talk to him. By the look of this woman, I guessed her to be my friend's wife, and I felt not a little tickled, remembering a similar house and a similar story in an old book of tales. Finding

my friend at last, I spent two nights with him. I left his house, however, on the third day, for I wanted to see the full moon of autumn at the port town of Tsuruga. Tōsai decided to accompany me, and walked into the road in high spirits, with the tails of his kimono tucked up in a somewhat strange way.

The white peak of Mount Shirane went out of sight at long last and the imposing figure of Mount Hina came in its stead. I crossed the bridge of Asamuzu and saw the famous reeds of Tamae, already coming into flower. Through the barrier-gate of Uguisu and the pass of Yunō, I came to the castle of Hiuchi, and hearing the cries of the early geese at the hill named Home-coming,[103] I entered the port of Tsuruga on the night of the fourteenth. The sky was clear and the moon was unusually bright. I said to the host of my inn, 'I hope it will be like this again tomorrow night when the full moon rises.' He answered, however, 'The weather of these northern districts is so changeable that, even with my experience, it is impossible to foretell the sky of tomorrow.' After a pleasant conversation with him over a bottle of wine, we went to the Myōjin Shrine of Kei, built to honour the soul of the Emperor Chūai.[104] The air of the shrine was hushed in the silence of night, and the moon through the dark needles of pine shone brilliantly upon the white sand in front of the altar, so that the ground seemed to have been covered with early frost. The host told me that it was the Bishop Yugyō II[105] who had first cut the grass, brought in sand and stones, and then dried the marshes around the shrine for the benefit of the worshippers, and that ever since it was the custom for the successors of the great bishop to bring a handful of sand upon the occasion of their visit to the shrine, the ritual being known as the sand-carrying ceremony of Yugyō.

> The moon was bright
> And divinely pure
> Upon the sand brought in
> By the Bishop Yugyō.

It rained on the night of the fifteenth, just as the host of my inn had predicted.

> The changeable sky
> Of the northern districts
> Prevented me from seeing
> The full moon of autumn.

It was again a fine day on the sixteenth. I went to the Coloured Beach[106] to pick up some pink shells. I sailed the distance of seven miles in a boat and arrived at the beach in no time, aided by a favourable wind. A man by the name of Tenya[107] accompanied me, with servants, food, drinks and everything else he could think of that we might need for our excursion. The beach was dotted with a number of fishermen's cottages and a tiny temple. As I sat in the temple, drinking warm tea and *sake*, I was overwhelmed by the loneliness of the evening scene.

> Lonelier I thought
> Than the Suma beach –
> The closing of autumn
> On the sea before me.

> Mingled with tiny shells
> I saw scattered petals
> Of bush-clovers
> Rolling with the waves.

I asked Tōsai to make a summary of the day's happenings and leave it at the temple as a souvenir.

As I returned to Tsuruga, Rotsū[108] met me and accompanied me to the province of Mino. When we entered the city of Ōgaki on horseback, Sora joined us again, having arrived from the province of Ise; Etsujin,[109] too, came hurrying on horseback, and we all went to the house of Jokō,[110] where I enjoyed reunion with Zensen,[111] Keikō,[112] his sons and many other old friends of mine who came to see me by day or by night. Everybody was overjoyed to see me as if I had returned unexpectedly from the dead. On

September the sixth, however, I left for the Ise Shrine, though the fatigue of the long journey was still with me, for I wanted to see the dedication of a new shrine there. As I stepped into a boat, I wrote:

> As firmly cemented clam-shells
> Fall apart in autumn,
> So I must take to the road again,
> Farewell, my friends.

Postscript

In this little book of travel is included everything under the sky – not only that which is hoary and dry but also that which is young and colourful, not only that which is strong and imposing but also that which is feeble and ephemeral. As we turn every corner of the Narrow Road to the Deep North, we sometimes stand up unawares to applaud and we sometimes fall flat to resist the agonizing pains we feel in the depths of our hearts. There are also times when we feel like taking to the road ourselves, seizing the raincoat lying near by, or times when we feel like sitting down till our legs take root, enjoying the scene we picture before our eyes. Such is the beauty of this little book that it can be compared to the pearls which are said to be made by the weeping mermaids in the far-off sea. What a travel it is indeed that is recorded in this book, and what a man he is who experienced it. The only thing to be regretted is that the author of this book, great man as he is, has in recent years grown old and infirm with hoary frost upon his eyebrows.

Early Summer of the Seventh Year of Genroku[113]
Soryū[114]

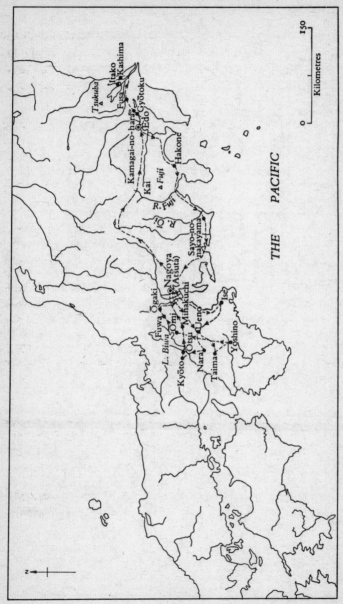

I

Tsukuba △
Itako
Fusa · Kashima
Gyōtoku
Edo
Kamagai-no-hara
Kai
△ Fuji
Hakone
R. Fuji
R. Ōi
Sayo-no-nakayama
Nagoya
Ogaki (Atsuta)
Fuwa
Ōmi
Mihakuchi
Ueno
L. Biwa
Ōtsu
Kyōto
Nara
Yoshino
Taima
Ise

THE PACIFIC

0   150
Kilometres

N

145

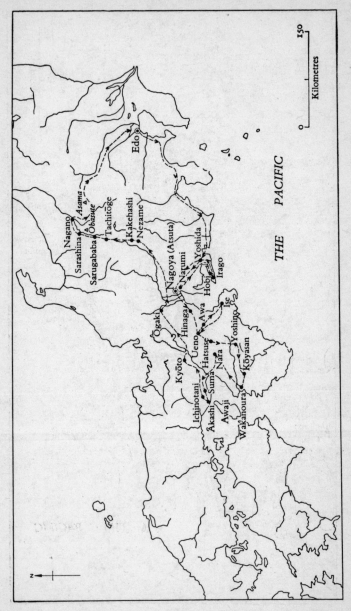

THE PACIFIC

150

Kilometres

0

Z

Edo

Asama
Obasute
Tachiōge
Kakehashi
Nezame
Yoshida
Nagano
Sarashina
Sarugababa
Nagoya (Atsuta)
Narumi
Irago
Hobi

Ōgaki
Hinaga
Ueno
Awa
Ise
Kyōto
Hatsuse
Nara
Yoshino
Ichinotani
Suma
Kōyasan
Akashi
Awaji
Wakanoura

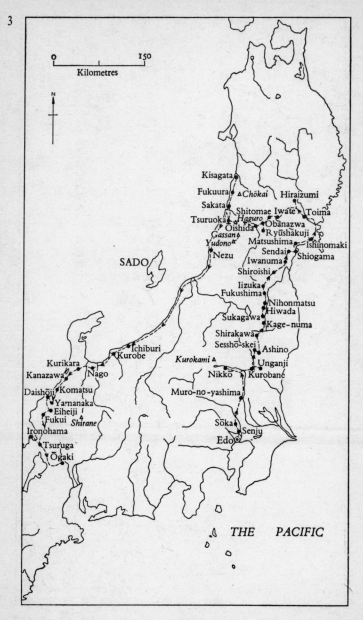

3

Kilometres

N

SADO

Kisagata
Fukuura △ *Chōkai*   Hiraizumi
Sakata
Shitomae Iwate   Toima
Tsuruoka *Haguro*   Obanazwa
Ōishida   Ryūshakuji
Gassan   Matsushima
Yudono   Ishinomaki
Nezu   Sendai   Shiogama
Iwanuma
Shiroishi
Iizuka
Fukushima
Nihonmatsu
Hiwada
Sukagawa   Kage-numa
Shirakawa
Sesshō-skei   Ashino
Ichiburi   *Kurokami* △   Unganji
Kurobe   Nikko   Kurobane
Kurikara
Kanazawa   Nago
Daishōji   Komatsu   Muro-no-yashima
Yamanaka
Eiheiji
Fukui   *Shirane*   Sōka
Ironohama   Edo   Senju
Tsuruga
Ōgaki

THE   PACIFIC

147

NOTES

1. Count the number of vowels to reckon syllables. The Japanese language falls most naturally into breathing groups of five or seven syllables.

2. This *haiku* is by Bashō, probably the best known of his master-pieces.

3. This *waka*, taken from *Manyō Shū*, is by Yamabe-no-Akahito, a nature poet in the years of Tempyō (729–48).

4. This *waka*, taken from *Kokin Shū*, is by Ki-no-Tomonori, a contemporary of Ki-no-Tsurayuki (868?–945).

5. This linked verse is taken from *Toshiyori Zuinō*. The first poem is by Ōshikōchi-no-Mitsune, a contemporary of Tsurayuki and the second is by Tsurayuki himself.

6. This linked verse is taken from *Shūi Shū*. The first poem is by an anonymous court lady and the second by Yoshimine-no-Munesada, who is better known as Henjō (816–90).

7. This linked verse is taken from *Kinyō Shū*. The first poem is by Eigen and the second by Eisei. These priests lived in the middle of the Heian period.

8. This linked verse is taken from *Ima Kagami*. The first poem is by Fujiwara-no-Kinnori (1103–80), the second by Minamoto-no-Arihito (1103–47) and the third by an anonymous woman.

9. This linked verse is by Sōgi and his disciples. The starting piece is by Sōgi himself (1421–1502), the second by Shōhaku (1443–1527), the third by Sōchō (1448–1532), and this order is followed in the part of the series quoted here.

10. This linked verse is taken from *Shinsen Inu-Tsukuba Shū* edited by Sōkan (dates unknown).

11. This linked verse is taken from *Moritake Dokugin*.

12. This linked verse is taken from *Gyokkai Shū*. The first poem is

by Seishō who is better known as Teishitsu (1610–73) and the second is by Teitoku (1571–1653).

13. This linked verse is by Sōin and his disciples. It is commonly known as *Danrin Toppyaku In*. The starting piece is by Sōin (1605–82), the second by Sessai, the third by Zaishiki (1643–1719), and the fourth by Ittetsu.

14. Hardly anything is known about this poet.

15. This linked verse is taken from *Edo Ryōgin*. The starting piece is by Bashō, the second by Shinshō who is better known as Sodō (1642–1716), the third again by Shinshō, and the fourth by Bashō.

16. Sampū (1647–1732) was a rich merchant in Edo, and acted in many ways as a financial supporter of Bashō. He was a good poet himself, whose style may be best represented by the following poem.

> Blinded by the glimmer
> Of the spade I am,
> As a farmer wields it
> In a spring field.

17. Bucchō (1643–1715) was the head priest of the Komponji Temple, twenty-first in descent from the founder. Bashō practised Zen under his guidance at the Chōkeiji Temple in Edo during the years of Empō and Tenna (1673–84).

18. Rokuso Gohei (dates unknown) was one of the pupils of Bucchō in Zen.

19. This linked verse, taken from *Fuyu no Hi*, is entitled 'the Wails of the Wind' ('*Kogarashi*'). The starting piece is by Bashō, the second by Yasui (1658–1743), the third by Kakei (1648–1716), and the fourth by Jūgo (1654–1717).

20. The disciple's name is Shikō (1665–1731). This passage is taken from *Kuzu no Matsubara*, a collection of his critical essays.

21. The disciple's name is Kikaku (1661–1707), probably the most important of Bashō's disciples. He is well known for the masculine sharpness of his wit and his habit of drinking. His style is probably best represented by the following poem:

> Locked firmly
> By a heavy bar –

This wooden door
Under the winter moon.

22. Kyorai (1651–1704) was a native of Nagasaki, whose importance as a disciple of Bashō is probably second only to Kikaku. A collection of his critical essays entitled *Kyorai Shō* is the most important source for Bashō's ideas on poetry. The style of his poetry is probably best represented by the following poem:

> Under the cherry
> Flower guards have assembled
> To chatter –
> Their hoary heads together.

23. Kyorai. This passage is taken from *Kyorai Shō*.

24. This passage, like the preceding one, is taken from *Kyorai Shō*. The linked verse quoted here is taken from *Izayoi Shū* edited by Ginboku. The first poem is by Ryūkō and the second by Shigenari.

25. This linked verse, taken from *Saru Mino*, is entitled 'The First Shower of Winter' ('*Hatsu Shigure*'). The starting piece is by Kyorai, the second by Bashō, the third by Bonchō (?–1714), the fourth by Fumiyuki, the fifth by Bashō, and the sixth by Kyorai.

26. The disciple's name is Shikō. This passage is taken from his *Oi Nikki*.

27. Buson (1716–83) is known as a painter as well as a *haiku* poet. Both the cover and the illustrations in the text of this book are by Buson.

THE RECORDS OF A WEATHER-EXPOSED SKELETON

1. Bashō is referring to Kōmon (Kuang-wên), a Chinese priest of the Nansung dynasty (1127–1279). His poem describing a state of ecstasy is collected in *Kōko Fūgetsu Shū* (*Chiang-hu Fêng-yüeh Chi*). A similar state of ecstasy is also recorded by Sōshi (Chuang Tzu).

2. 1684. All the dates in the text, including months and seasons, are to be interpreted in the light of the old lunar calendar in use during the lifetime of Bashō, in which January began roughly one month later than it does in the present calendar. In the same way, the units of

distance used in the text refer to Japanese units. A mile, for example, is a Japanese mile, which is approximately two British miles.

3. Chiri (1648–1716), a native of Yamato (Nara Prefecture), lived most of his life in Asakusa in the city of Edo (Tokyo).

4. This *haiku* is in the irregular form of seven–seven–five.

5. This *haiku* is in the irregular form of seven–eight–five.

6. Toboku or Tu Mu (803–52) is a Chinese poet of the late Tang dynasty. Bashō is referring to his poem entitled 'Early Morning Departure'.

7. Fūbaku (dates unknown) was a *haiku* poet in Ise (Mie Prefecture). His teacher Isshō (1643–1707), a physician in Edo, probably gave Bashō a letter of introduction.

8. This *haiku* is in the irregular form of seven–seven–five.

9. Saigyō (1118–90) is an outstanding nature poet of the late Heian period. He started his life as a minor *samurai* in the court of ex-Emperor Toba (1103–56), but at the age of twenty-three, he suddenly abandoned both the court and his family, and lived as a wandering poet for the rest of his life. Frequent references to him by Bashō throughout the travel sketches reveal that Bashō always took him as a model in life and poetry. To quote just one poem from his anthology, *Sanka Shū*:

> My sincere hope is
> To leave the world in spring
> Under the blooming cherry –
> In February, if possible,
> On the eve of the full moon.

This hope of his was, in fact, realized, for he died on February the sixteenth in 1190.

10. This *haiku* is in the irregular form of eight–seven–five.

11. Urashima is a legendary figure, a young fisherman who rescues a turtle on the beach, visits the palace of a sea-goddess, stays there for many years as her guest, and returns to find the world completely changed. His loneliness induces him to open a *tamatebako*, a small box given him by the sea-goddess as a gift, and as a line of smoke rises from the box, he is changed into an aged man with hoary hair.

12. This *haiku* is in the irregular form of eight–seven–five.

13. Rozan or Lü-shan is a body of mountains in the Kiangsi province in China. Many poets sought seclusion in these mountains, among them Hui–yüan (334–416) and Po Chü-i (772–846).

14. This *haiku* is in the irregular form of six–eight–five.

15. This *haiku* is in the irregular form of six–eight–five.

16. Hakui or Po-i is an ancient sage of China. He advised Wu-wang of the Chou dynasty not to murder Chou–wang of the Yin dynasty for it was against the principle of loyalty, but, his advice ignored, he sought complete seclusion in the mountains.

17. Kyoyū or Hsu Yu is an ancient hermit of China. When Emperor Yao said he would give him his kingdom, he fled at once and washed out his ears in the water of the River Ying Shui.

18. Godaigo (1288–1339) was the ninety-sixth emperor of Japan. He died in the mountains of Yoshino after a stormy life.

19. This *haiku* is in the irregular form of eight-seven-five. The Japanese name of the weed 'reminiscence' is shinobu, whose Latin name is *davallia bullata*.

20. Lady Tokiwa (dates unknown) was the ill-fated mistress of Minamoto-no-Yoshitomo (see below), mother of Yoshitsune. She is said to have been murdered by a band of robbers while on her way from Kyōto to the eastern provinces after her husband's death.

21. Minamoto-no-Yoshitomo (1123–60) fought against his own father and killed him in the Battle of Hogen in 1156, but suffered a serious defeat in the Battle of Heiji fought two years after and was murdered in flight.

22. Moritake (1473–1549), a priest of the Ise Shrine, is one of the early innovators of linked verse of a lower order. For details, see p. 15.

23. Bokuin (1646–1725) was a shipping agent in Ōgaki. His poetic style is probably best represented by the following poem:

> As if to show
> In dancing sprays
> The coolness of summer,
> A water mill revolves.

24. Chikusai is the hero of a comic story by that name, attributed to Karasuma Mitsuhiro (1579–1638). Chikusai is a quack more experienced in provoking laughter than in medicine.

25. This *haiku* is in the irregular form of eight–seven–five.

26. This *haiku* is in the irregular form of five–five–seven.

27. The water-drawing ceremony or Omizutori is performed in February at Tōdaiji in Nara. The water drawn at this mid-winter ceremony is believed to have a mystical power of purification.

28. Shūfū (1646–1717) was a rich merchant in Kyōto. His villa at Narutaki was a favourite haunt of the poets.

29. Ninkō (1606–86), better known as the priest Hōyo, was the third head priest of the Saiganji Temple.

30. This *haiku* is in the irregular form of six–eight–five.

31. Bashō is referring to Tohō (1657–1730), a native of Iga (Mie Prefecture), whose collection of critical essays entitled *Sanzōshi* is an important source for Bashō's ideas on poetry.

32. Daiten (1629–85) was the hundred and sixty-third head priest of the Engakuji Temple in Kamakura. Kikaku practised Zen under his guidance.

33. See note 21 to Introduction.

34. Tokoku (?–1690), a merchant in Nagoya, was a special favourite of Bashō among his disciples. His early death was bitterly deplored by Bashō.

35. Tōyō (?–1712) was an inn-keeper in Atsuta.

36. This *haiku* is in the irregular form of five–eight–eight.

A VISIT TO THE KASHIMA SHRINE

1. Teishitsu (1610–73), a merchant in Kyōto, was a disciple of Teitoku. He is the editor of *Gyokkai Shū*.

2. Chūnagon is a popular name of Arihara-no-Yukihira (818–93). Teishitsu is referring to his famous poem:

> Should anyone ask you
> Where I could be,
> Tell him I am all by myself
> Shedding salt tears by the salt farms
> On the Suma Beach.

3. See note 13 to *The Records of a Weather-exposed Skeleton*.

4. Ransetsu (1654–1707) was a minor *samurai* in Edo, known for his extremely carefree manner of living. His poetic style is probably best represented by the following poem he wrote shortly before his death:

> A single leaf –
> Just a single leaf has fallen,
> And was swept away breathless
> By a gust of wild wind.

5. Yamatotakeru (dates unknown) was an ancient prince of Japan, noted for chivalric valour. He is believed to be the son of Emperor Keikō, the twelfth emperor of Japan. Bashō is referring to the following poem of his recorded in *Kojiki*.

> How many days and nights
> Have we slept on the road
> Since we left behind
> Niibari and Mount Tsukuba?   *Yamatotakeru*

> If I remember aright
> Nine nights we have slept
> And ten days we have toiled
> Travelling on the road.   *An old man*

6. The first anthology of linked verse was published in 1356 by Nijō Yoshimoto (1320–88) under the title of *Tsukuba Shū*.

7. Tachibana-no-Tamenaka (?–1085) is a poet of the late Heian period. This episode of his is recorded in *Mumyōshō* by Kamo-no-Chōmei (1153–1216).

8. Bashō is referring to Seishōnagon. The story of her disappointment is recorded in her *Makura-no-Sōshi*.

9. Tōsei is Bashō's earlier pen name. See p. 23.

10. Sora (1649–1710), a native of Shinano (Nagano Prefecture), accompanied Bashō not only on the present trip but also on the journey of *The Narrow Road to the Deep North*. His *Zuikō Ki* is of great importance in the analysis of the fictitious elements in the greatest of Bashō's travel sketches.

11. Sōha (dates unknown) is generally believed to have been the head priest of the Jyōrinji Temple in Edo.

12. Jijun (1623–97) was a physician in Edo. He was living in seclusion at Itako when Bashō visited him.

13. 1687.

THE RECORDS OF A TRAVEL-WORN SATCHEL

1. See note 9 to *The Records of a Weather-exposed Skeleton*.

2. Sōgi (1421–1502) is generally believed to have been the greatest master in linked verse of a higher order. He is the editor of *Shinsen Tsukuba Shū*. See p. 13.

3. Sesshū (1420–1506), a native of Bizen (Okayama Prefecture), was the greatest painter of the Muromachi period. He painted nature in black and white with superb masculine strokes of the brush.

4. Rikyū (1522–91), a native of Sakai (Ōsaka), was the greatest master in tea ceremony during the Muromachi period.

5. *Camellia sasanqua*.

6. Chōtarō (dates unknown) was a *samurai* in the service of Lord Rosen. See note 8, below, for Rosen.

7. See note 21 to Introduction.

8. Rosen (1655–1733) whose real name was Naitō Yoshihide, was the feudal lord of Taira in the province of Iwaki (Fukushima Prefecture). He was a disciple of Sōin in poetry.

9. Ki-no-Tsurayuki (859–945) was one of the outstanding poets of the Heian period. He was the editor of *Kokin Shū*. He wrote the diary named *Tosa Nikki* under the disguise of a court lady.

10. Kamo-no-Chōmei (1153–1216) was a priest of the Kamakura period. He spent most of his life in seclusion. Bashō is referring to his *Hōjō Ki*.

11. Abutsu (1228?–83), the second wife of Fujiwara-no-Tameie (1198–1275), became a nun after her husband's death. She wrote *Izayoi Nikki* on her way from Kyōto to Kamakura.

12. The Japanese name of the promontory is Hoshizaki.

13. Asukai Masaaki (1611–79) was a poet of the Edo period. He is reported to have said, 'Speak directly from your heart when you write poetry'.

Notes

14. See note 34 to *The Records of a Weather-exposed Skeleton*.

15. Etsujin (1656–?) was a dyer in Nagoya. He accompanied Bashō on the trip to the village of Sarashina.

16. *Manyō Shū* is the first major anthology of Japanese poetry, consisting of twenty volumes. Poems included in this anthology were written over the period of more than four hundred years between the reign of Nintoku, the sixteenth emperor, and that of Kōken, the forty-sixth emperor. The account of Irago promontory is to be found in Volume 1.

17. *Go* is an oriental game resembling draughts. It is played with small black and white counters of polished stone on a thick wooden board.

18. Bashō is referring to Sōgi, whose poem on Kuwana is recorded by Saikaku. For Sōgi, see note 2, above.

19. The Japanese name of this pass is Tsue-tsuki-zaka.

20. Shunjō (1121–1206) is better known as Chōgen. His life work was the restoration of the Daibutsu Den at Tōdaiji Temple in Nara.

21. Ryū Shōsha (1616–93) was a priest of the Ise Shrine. He was a noted scholar of his day.

22. Ajiro Minbu (1640–83) was a priest of the Ise Shrine. His son Hirokazu (1657–1717) wrote *haiku* under the pen name Setsudō.

23. Bashō is referring to Tokoku. See note 34 to *The Records of a Weather-exposed Skeleton*.

24. The Japanese name of this waterfall is Ryūmon.

25. The Japanese name of this plant is *asunaro* (hatched-leaved arbor-vitae).

26. Sesshōkō is a popular name of Fujiwara-no-Yoshitsune (1169–1206), for he was appointed a regent (*sesshō*) by ex-Emperor Gotoba. His poem on Yoshino is to be found in *Shin Kokin Shū*.

27. Bashō is referring to the Priest Shōkū (1177–1248), the founder the Seizan sect. The story of his fall from his horse is recorded by Kenkō (1283–1350) in his *Tsurezure Gusa*.

28. Ganjin or Chien-chen (688–763) is a Chinese priest, the founder of the Tendai sect in Japan. He built Tōshōdaiji Temple in Nara.

29. See note 2 to *A Visit to the Kashima Shrine*.

30. Bashō is referring to the Battle of Ichi-no-tani fought in 1184, when, by a surprise attack, a relatively small band of soldiers under the command of Minamoto-no-Yoshitsune won a devastating victory over the big army of the Heike clan.

31. Bashō is thinking of Tu Fu's poem on Tung-ting Hu, a lake in the Hunan province of China.

32. Matsukaze and Murasame were women of low birth, engaged in fishing on the Suma beach, but they met Arihara-no-Yukihira during his exile and became his mistresses. Their misfortune in love is the subject of the *nō* play entitled *Matsukaze*.

33. The Japanese name of this precipice is Hachibuse Nozoki.

34. The Japanese name of this precipice is Saka Otoshi.

35. Yoshitsune (1159–89) was the most colourful and yet at the same time the most tragic hero of the Minamotos (Genji). When separated from his mother (see note 20 to *The Records of a Weather-exposed Skeleton*), he went to the Kuramadera Temple in Kyōto, practised military arts in secret, helped his brother Yoritomo (1147–99) to win a victory over the Tairas (Heike), but, having provoked his displeasure, was forced to seek exile in the north, where he met a heroic death, fighting against the army of Fujiwara-no-Yasuhira who had betrayed him.

A VISIT TO SARASHINA VILLAGE

1. See note 15 to *The Records of a Travel-worn Satchel*.

2. Kakei (1648–1716) was a physician in Nagoya. The style of his poetry is probably best represented by the following poem.

> Broken to pieces
> By a winter storm,
> A two-day-old
> New moon in the sky.

THE NARROW ROAD TO THE DEEP NORTH

1. *Moxa* is the dried leaf of *artemisia moxa*. It is applied to the skin in small bits and ignited. It is generally believed to have curative effects for all kinds of diseases.

Notes

2. See note 16 to Introduction.

3. The Festival of Dolls (*hina matsuri*) is celebrated on 3 March. It is sometimes called the Festival of Peach Blossoms, or simply, Girls' Festival.

4. 1689.

5. See note 10 to *A Visit to the Kashima Shrine*.

6. The Japanese name of this goddess is Ko-no-Hana Sakuya Hime. Her husband's name is Ninigi-no-Mikoto. Refer to *Kojiki* for the details of Japanese mythology.

7. The Japanese name of this god is Hohodemi-no-Mikoto.

8. Kūkai (774–835) is better known as Kōbō Daishi. He is the founder of the Shingon sect and the builder of the temples at Kōya-san. The temple at Nikkō, however, was founded not by Kūkai but by Shōdō (737–817). The temple enjoyed unusual prosperity under the protection of the Tokugawas.

9. The Japanese name of this waterfall is Urami-no-taki.

10. Jōbōji Takakatsu (1658–1730) was a high-ranking *samurai* in the service of Ōzeki Masutsune.

11. Tōsui (1662–1728) was a younger brother of Jōbōji Takakatsu. His real name was Kanokobata Toyoaki. According to Sora, his pen name was Suitō rather than Tōsui.

12. Dog-shooting (*inu oumono*) was a sport invented in the beginning of the Kamakura period, probably for the purpose of practising archery. It went out of fashion, however, rather quickly.

13. Lady Tamamo is generally believed to have been a fox in disguise. She became a favourite of Emperor Konoe (1139–55), but her disguise being suspected by a priest, she fled to the northern provinces, and finally transformed herself into a poisonous rock (Sesshō-seki). See note 19, below.

14. Nasu-no-Yoichi (dates unknown) was a minor *samurai* in the service of the Minamotos. He succeeded in shooting a fan suspended high over a drifting boat in the Battle of Yashima in 1185, a feat that made him famous throughout the country.

15. The founder of the Shugen sect was En-no-Otsunu, popularly known as En-no-Gyōja, a priest of the seventh to eighth century.

16. See note 17 to Introduction.

17. Genmyō or Yuan-miao (1238–95) was a Chinese priest of the Nan-sung dynasty. He confined himself for fifteen years in a cave, which he named Death Gate.

18. Hōun or Fa-yun (466–529) was a Chinese priest of the Liang dynasty. He spent most of his life preaching from the tiny hut which he had built on a high rock.

19. The Japanese name of this stone is Sesshō-seki.

20. Bashō is referring to the following poem by Saigyō in *Shin Kokin Shū*.

> Under this solitary willow
> Spreading its grateful shade
> Over the crystal stream,
> Let us rest our tired legs
> On our way to the North.

For Saigyō, refer to note 9 to *The Records of a Weather-exposed Skeleton*.

21. The Latin name of this plant is *deutzia crenata*.

22. Fujiwara-no-Kiyosuke (1104–77) is a poet-scholar of the Heian period. Bashō is referring to his *Fukuro Zōshi*.

23. The Japanese name of this pond is Kage-numa.

24. Tōkyū (1638–1715) was an influential official in the post town of Sukagawa.

25. Gyōki Bosatsu (668–749) was a priest of the Nara period. He devoted his whole life to the salvation of the common people.

26. The Japanese name of this place is Tsuki-no-wa.

27. The Japanese name of this post town is Se-no-ue.

28. Satō Motoharu (?–1189) was the father of Tsugunobu (1158–85) and Tadanobu (1161–86) who fought bravely for Yoshitsune. Motoharu himself fought for Yoshitsune against the army of Yoritomo. After the death of Tsugunobu and Tadanobu, their wives wore armour to console their aged mothers left behind.

29. Bashō is referring to the tombstone of Yang Hu (221–78), which was named the Weeping Tombstone by Tu Yu (222–84) because there was not a single person who could refrain from weeping in its presence.

30. See note 35 to *The Records of a Travel-worn Satchel*.

31. Benkei (dates unknown) was a priest more interested in military feats than in preaching. He served Yoshitsune with the utmost devotion after he was subdued by him in a fight.

32. The May Festival is celebrated on the fifth of May. It is sometimes called the Festival of the Iris, or simply, Boys' Festival.

33. Fujiwara-no-Sanekata (?–998) was a poet of the Heian period. He had a quarrel with Fujiwara-no-Yukinari (972–1027) at court, and was ordered by the emperor to go to the northern provinces in exile. He passed by the road-side image of a god without dismounting, however, and was punished at once by a fatal fall from his horse.

34. Nōin Hōshi (988–?) was one of the outstanding poets of the Heian period. He is believed to have had a deep influence on Saigyō.

35. Kyohaku (?–1696) was one of Bashō's disciples in Edo.

36. Kaemon (1665–1746) was not only a painter but also sculptor and poet. His son wrote poetry under the pen name of Hakkyo.

37. 724.

38. Ōno-no-Azumabito was a general who subjugated the northern provinces by the order of Fujiwara-no-Umakai (694–737).

39. 762.

40. Emi-no-Asakari (?–764) was the son of Emi-no-Oshikatsu. Both the father and the son rebelled against Emperor Kōken and were killed in a fight.

41. Shōmu (701–56) was the forty-fifth emperor of Japan.

42. The Japanese name of this rock is Oki–no–ishi.

43. The stories of Heike (*Heike Monogatari*) are often recited to the lute by minstrels.

44. Izumi-no-Saburō (1167–89) is better known as Fujiwara-no-Tadahira. He was killed by his brother who betrayed him and Yoshitsune. See note 56, below.

45. 1187.

46. Dōtei or Tung-ting Hu is a lake in the Hunan province of China.

47. Seiko or Si Hu is a lake in the Chekiang province of China.

48. Sekkō or Tsien-tang kiang is a river in the Chekiang province of China.

49. Ungo (1582–1659) was a priest of the Myōshinji Temple in Kyōto. He rebuilt the Zuiganji Temple at Matsushima in 1636.

50. Sodō (1642–1716) is a native of Kai (Yamanashi Prefecture). He was well versed in the Chinese classics. His poetic style is probably best represented by the following poem:

> Fresh green for my eye,
> In the mountains, for my ear
> The songs of cuckoo –
> First bonito for my tongue.

51. Hara Anteki (dates unknown) was a physician in Edo.

52. Dakushi (dates unknown) was a native of Ōgaki. He lived in Edo as a minor *samurai*.

53. Makabe-no-Heishirō (dates unknown), better known as Hōshin, was a priest of the Kamakura period.

54. Kenbutsu (dates unknown) was a priest of the Heian period. He is said to have confined himself in a tiny temple at Matsushima for twelve years.

55. Bashō is referring to the following poem by Ōtomo-no-Yakamochi (718–85):

> As if to celebrate
> The peaceful reign of our prince,
> A mountain was discovered
> In the north of our country
> Blooming with flowers of gold.

56. Bashō is referring to Fujiwara-no-Kiyohira (1056–1128), Motohira (dates unknown), and Hidehira (?–1187). These three able men succeeded in creating the so-called golden age of the North. Hidehira's son, Yasuhira (?–1189), however, fought against his own brother, Tadahira (1167–89) and killed him, but was killed, in turn, by Minamoto-no-Yoritomo. Thus the golden age of the North came to an end after a brief period of prosperity.

57. Kanefusa (1127–89) was a faithful retainer of Yoshitsune. He fought very bravely in spite of his old age.

58. The Japanese name of this chapel is Hikari Dō or Konjiki Dō.

59. Seifū (1651–1721) was a merchant in Obanazawa. He often visited Bashō in Edo on his business trips.

60. Jikaku (794–864), better known as Ennin, was a priest of the Tendai sect. He founded Ryūshakuji in 860.

61. The Japanese name is Goten.

62. The Japanese name is Hayabusa.

63. The Japanese name of this cascade is Shiraito-no-taki.

64. Zushi Sakichi (?–1693) was a dyer in the village of Tamuke in the province of Dewa (Yamagata Prefecture). He wrote poetry under the pen name Rogan.

65. Egaku (?–1707) was the acting bishop between 1687 and 1691. He died at the Kegonji Temple in the province of Mino (Gifu Prefecture).

66. Nōjo (dates unknown) is generally believed to have been the third son of Emperor Sushun (?–592).

67. *Court Ceremonies and Rites during the Years of Engi* (*Engishiki*) is the book of law consisting of fifty volumes, compiled by Fuji-wara-no-Tokihira (871–909) and others by the order of Emperor Daigo. There is, however, no entry about the shrine on Mount Sato in this book.

68. Tendai sect was first brought to Japan by Ganjin (688–763). Saichyō (767–822) made it an important sect in Japan. It places a great deal of emphasis on rites and rituals.

69. Gassan (dates unknown) was a famous swordsmith during the years of Kenkyū (1190–98).

70. Ryōsen or Lung-chüan was a spring in the Chekiang province in China.

71. Kanshō or Kanchiang was a famous swordsmith of the Wu dynasty. Both he and his wife, Bakuya (Muyeh), were noted for their skill.

72. Bashō is referring to a poem by Chên Yü-i, a poet of the Sung dynasty. Bashō is reported to have said, 'My art is something like a furnace in summer and a fan in winter'.

73. Gyōson (?–1135) was a priest of the Heian period. Bashō is referring to the following poem of his in *Kinyō Shū*.

> What a pity it is
> There is in the mountains
> Not a person to admire

This beautiful cherry
In glorious bloom.

74. Nagayama Shigeyuki (dates unknown) was a *samurai* in the service of the Sakai family who ruled the town of Tsuruoka for generations.

75. Fugyoku (?–1697) was a physician in Sakata. His poems with Bashō's critical comments were published under the title *Aki no Yo*.

76. See note 34, above.

77. Bashō is referring to the following poem by Saigyō:

> Buried in the waves
> So that it seems
> Fishermen's boats are sailing
> Over the waves of blossoms –
> A cherry tree at Kisagata.

78. Empress Jingū is generally believed to have ruled Japan in the second half of the fourth century. She made an unsuccessful attempt to subject Korea.

79. Lady Seishi or Hsi-shih is known for her melancholy beauty. She was sent to Fu-chai of the Wu dynasty by Kou-chien of the Yüeh dynasty as a gift.

80. Teiji (dates unknown) was a merchant in the province of Mino (Gifu Prefecture). He was a disciple of Gonsui in poetry.

81. Bashō is referring to the seventh of July when it is believed that the two stars named Shepherd (Altair) and Weaver (Vega), normally separated by the Milky Way, meet for their annual rendezvous in the sky. This special day is celebrated as Tanabata in Japan.

82. The Japanese name is Oyashirazu.

83. The Japanese name is Koshirazu.

84. The Japanese name is Inumodori.

85. The Japanese name is Komagaeshi.

86. The sea off the coast of Toyama Prefecture is called the Angry Sea (Ariso Umi) because of its roughness.

87. Kasho (?–1731) was a merchant in Ōsaka. He wrote the

following poem to deplore the death of Isshō. For Isshō, see the next note.

> In the autumn wind
> There will at least be
> A lotus to sit upon
> For eternal peace.

88. Isshō (1653–88) was a promising poet in Kanazawa, but died at the age of thirty-five. He is said to have written the following poem shortly before his death.

> How beautiful it is,
> The snow on the ground,
> And the cloud in the west
> That brings more of it.

89. The Japanese name is Komatsu.

90. Saitō Sanemori (1111--83) was originally in the service of the Minamotos, but later he was taken into the service of the Tairas. When he went to the Battle of Shinohara at the age of seventy-three, he dyed his hair to conceal his age, but he was killed by Tezuka Mitsumori.

91. See note 21 to *The Records of a Weather-exposed Skeleton*.

92. The Minamotos were the descendants of Emperor Saga (786–842). They formed a clan (Genji) and their political power reached its height under Yoritomo (1147–99). They were opposed by the Tairas, the descendants of Emperor Kanmu (737–806), who formed another clan (Heike). The political power of the Tairas reached its height under Kiyomori (1118–81).

93. Kiso Yoshinaka (1154–84) was one of the leaders of the Minamotos. He excelled in military power but lacked political shrewdness.

94. Higuchi-no-Jirō (dates unknown) was one of the so-called four guardians of Yoshinaka. He was a former friend of Sanemori.

95. Kazan (968–1008) was the sixty-fifth emperor of Japan.

96. It is generally believed either Bashō or the scribe misspelled the name of this hot spring. Bashō is probably referring to the Arima hot spring in Hyōgo Prefecture.

97. Kumenosuke (1676–1751) was an inn-keeper at Yamanaka. He wrote *haiku* under the pen name, Tōyō. His father, Matabei, wrote poetry under the pen name, Takenori.

98. See note 1 to *A Visit to the Kashima Shrine*.

99. Teitoku (1571–1653) was a master of linked verse of a lower order in Kyōto. He was not only a good poet but also a good scholar. For his poetic style, see p. 16.

100. Hokushi (?–1718) was a sword sharpener in Kanazawa. His house was burned down in 1690, when he wrote the following poem. Bashō praised it highly in his letter of condolence.

> My house is burned,
> But the cherry tree in my garden
> Scatters its blossoms
> As if nothing had happened.

101. Dōgen (1200–53) was the founder of the Sōtō sect. He built the Eiheiji Temple and preached the doctrines of Zen.

102. Tōsai (dates unknown) was a native of Fukui. His poems are to be found in *Shinzoku Inu-Tsukuba Shū* edited by Kigin (1624–1750).

103. The Japanese name of this hill is Kaeru-yama.

104. Chūai (dates unknown) was the fourteenth emperor of Japan. He was the husband of Empress Jingū.

105. Yugyō II (1237–1319) was known as Taa Shōnin. He was the successor of Ippen Shōnin (1239–89), the founder of the Ji sect.

106. The Japanese name of this beach is Iro-no-hama.

107. Tenya Gorōemon (dates unknown) was a shipper in Tsuruga.

108. Rotsū (1651?–1739), like Izen (?–1711), was famous for the eccentricity of his life. He started as a priest, but, reduced to beggary, he wandered all over the country. His self-indulgence sometimes incurred criticism from other disciples. The following poem of his, however, was used by Bashō as an example of *hosomi* (slenderness).

> Waterfowl, too,
> Must be fast asleep
> In this hushed silence
> Of Lake Yogo.

109. See note 15 to *The Records of a Travel-worn Satchel*.

110. Jokō (dates unknown) was a minor *samurai* in Ōgaki. He was retired from his service when Bashō visited him.

111. Zensen (dates unknown) was a high ranking *samurai* in Ōgaki.

112. Keikō (1673–1735), a *samurai* in Ōgaki, had three sons, named Shikin, Sensen and Bunchō.

113. 1694.

114. Soryū (dates unknown) is generally believed to have been a priest and scholar in Edo. A clean copy of the final draft of *The Narrow Road to the Deep North* was made by him at Bashō's request.

FOR THE BEST IN PAPERBACKS, LOOK FOR THE (🐧)

In every corner of the world, on every subject under the sun, Penguin represents quality and variety – the very best in publishing today.

For complete information about books available from Penguin – including Pelicans, Puffins, Peregrines and Penguin Classics – and how to order them, write to us at the appropriate address below. Please note that for copyright reasons the selection of books varies from country to country.

In the United Kingdom: For a complete list of books available from Penguin in the U.K., please write to *Dept E.P., Penguin Books Ltd, Harmondsworth, Middlesex, UB7 0DA*

In the United States: For a complete list of books available from Penguin in the U.S., please write to *Dept BA, Penguin, 299 Murray Hill Parkway, East Rutherford, New Jersey 07073*

In Canada: For a complete list of books available from Penguin in Canada, please write to *Penguin Books Canada Ltd, 2801 John Street, Markham, Ontario L3R 1B4*

In Australia: For a complete list of books available from Penguin in Australia, please write to the *Marketing Department, Penguin Books Australia Ltd, P.O. Box 257, Ringwood, Victoria 3134*

In New Zealand: For a complete list of books available from Penguin in New Zealand, please write to the *Marketing Department, Penguin Books (NZ) Ltd, Private Bag, Takapuna, Auckland 9*

In India: For a complete list of books available from Penguin, please write to *Penguin Overseas Ltd, 706 Eros Apartments, 56 Nehru Place, New Delhi, 110019*

In Holland: For a complete list of books available from Penguin in Holland, please write to *Penguin Books Nederland B.V., Postbus 195, NL–1380AD Weesp, Netherlands*

In Germany: For a complete list of books available from Penguin, please write to *Penguin Books Ltd, Friedrichstrasse 10 – 12, D–6000 Frankfurt Main 1, Federal Republic of Germany*

In Spain: For a complete list of books available from Penguin in Spain, please write to *Longman Penguin España, Calle San Nicolas 15, E–28013 Madrid, Spain*

FOR THE BEST IN PAPERBACKS, LOOK FOR THE 🐧

PENGUIN BOOKS OF POETRY

American Verse
Ballads
British Poetry Since 1945
Caribbean Verse
A Choice of Comic and Curious Verse
Contemporary American Poetry
Contemporary British Poetry
Eighteenth-Century Verse
Elizabethan Verse
English Poetry 1918–60
English Romantic Verse
English Verse
First World War Poetry
Georgian Poetry
Irish Verse
Light Verse
London in Verse
Love Poetry
The Metaphysical Poets
Modern African Poetry
Modern Arab Poetry
New Poetry
Poems of Science
Poetry of the Thirties
Post-War Russian Poetry
Spanish Civil War Verse
Unrespectable Verse
Victorian Verse
Women Poets

PENGUIN CLASSICS

THE LIBRARY OF EVERY CIVILIZED PERSON

Saint Anselm	**The Prayers and Meditations**
Saint Augustine	**The Confessions**
Bede	**A History of the English Church and People**
Chaucer	**The Canterbury Tales**
	Love Visions
	Troilus and Criseyde
Froissart	**The Chronicles**
Geoffrey of Monmouth	**The History of the Kings of Britain**
Gerald of Wales	**History and Topography of Ireland**
	The Journey through Wales and **The Description of Wales**
Gregory of Tours	**The History of the Franks**
Julian of Norwich	**Revelations of Divine Love**
William Langland	**Piers the Ploughman**
Sir John Mandeville	**The Travels of Sir John Mandeville**
Marguerite de Navarre	**The Heptameron**
Christine de Pisan	**The Treasure of the City of Ladies**
Marco Polo	**The Travels**
Richard Rolle	**The Fire of Love**
Thomas à Kempis	**The Imitation of Christ**

ANTHOLOGIES AND ANONYMOUS WORKS

The Age of Bede
Alfred the Great
Beowulf
A Celtic Miscellany
The Cloud of Unknowing and Other Works
The Death of King Arthur
The Earliest English Poems
Early Christian Writings
Early Irish Myths and Sagas
Egil's Saga
The Letters of Abelard and Heloise
Medieval English Verse
Njal's Saga
Seven Viking Romances
Sir Gawain and the Green Knight
The Song of Roland

PENGUIN CLASSICS

THE LIBRARY OF EVERY CIVILIZED PERSON

Pedro de Alarcon	**The Three-Cornered Hat and Other Stories**
Leopoldo Alas	**La Regenta**
Ludovico Ariosto	**Orlando Furioso**
Giovanni Boccaccio	**The Decameron**
Baldassar Castiglione	**The Book of the Courtier**
Benvenuto Cellini	**Autobiography**
Miguel de Cervantes	**Don Quixote**
	Exemplary Stories
Dante	**The Divine Comedy** (in 3 volumes)
	La Vita Nuova
Bernal Diaz	**The Conquest of New Spain**
Carlo Goldoni	**Four Comedies (The Venetian Twins / The Artful Widow / Mirandolina / The Superior Residence)**
Niccolo Machiavelli	**The Discourses**
	The Prince
Alessandro Manzoni	**The Betrothed**
Giorgio Vasari	**Lives of the Artists** (in 2 volumes)

and

Five Italian Renaissance Comedies (Machiavelli / The Mandragola; Ariosto / Lena; Aretino / The Stablemaster; Gl'Intronatie / The Deceived; Guarini / The Faithful Shepherd)

The Jewish Poets of Spain

The Poem of the Cid

Two Spanish Picaresque Novels (Anon / Lazarille de Tormes; de Quevedo / The Swindler)